High praise for *The Smart Real Estate Investor's Guide*:

"Karim Jaude is 'my partner in real estate.' This book represents learning gleaned from a lifetime spent making real estate deals of almost every kind. It is rare that you find a book in which the author is not trying to sell you some 'program' where he profits not from the deals you invest in together but from getting you to buy a 'system.' The 'Jaude Principles' in this book are all the system you will need. Now, go use them!"

—*Patrick A. Fraioli, Patent/Corporate/Litigation Attorney*

"Truly one of the best real estate books I have ever read. I just could not put it down . . . . A well written book, by a well seasoned professional. A must-read for any real estate investor."

—*M. Hossein Khoylow, Real Estate Broker, Investor*

Even higher praise for Karim Jaude's skills as a real estate investor:

"Karim Jaude has had to make his fortune from scratch three different times in three different countries due to his dislocation from turbulent politics in Lebanon and Iran. In two decades in the USA, he has again risen to outstanding success—a tribute to his business acumen and his grasp of what makes real estate investors into millionaires. He is a master of deal-making, both on the buy and on the sell."

—Kevin Davis, Commercial Real Estate Syndicator

"Karim Jaude was my real estate partner for ten years. His integrity, professionalism, and knowledge of real estate are among the best I have ever seen. His attention to detail and his ability to find, acquire, and manage challenging properties separates him from everyone else."

—*Richard Citron, Business/Corporate Attorney*

Seldom do you come across people of Karim Jaude's caliber and character. Knowing Karim for over four years, investing with and learning from his profound real estate experiences, I have come to appreciate his market brilliance as well as admire his integrity and sincerity! I consider Karim my mentor, an excellent networking guru, and above all a true friend!"

—Mark Fotohabadi, Real Estate Finance Broker, Investor

"During the past three years I have purchased three properties in Texas and Colorado with Karim Jaude's help. To this day I have never personally been to Texas or Colorado. Karim's all-inclusive service makes it easy for busy investors like me. Karim and his team took care of every detail, including writing the sales contract, finding the right mortgage, overseeing the property inspection, and ensuring a timely closing. Most importantly, Karim was able to negotiate deals for immediate profit. On my last transaction, the property appraised for more than the sales price; I had already made $10,000 before the close of escrow."

—*Babak Moghaddam, Real Estate Mortgage Broker, Investor*

"It is possible to write an entire book strictly singing the praises of Karim Jaude. First and foremost, he is a man of the utmost integrity. He has consistently displayed the rare quality of putting the needs and interests of others before his own. I've known him personally for over a decade and have participated in many business endeavors with him. Every experience with him would get an A+ in terms of how well our projects have performed, in terms of his understanding of my objectives, and in terms of the quality of the other professionals he has incorporated into the process. I'm proud to call him my friend and lucky to consider him a mentor."

—*Corey Nathan, Business Consultant, Real Estate Investor*

"[Karim's seminars are] a comfortable and friendly forum that I continually use to obtain some of my CPE requirements as a CPA. Karim is very knowledgeable, and he consistently uses quality panelists in conducting his seminars. Through his seminars, I have also been able to obtain new clients. Talk about providing more than expected. It is wonderful."

—*Soheil Rabbani, CPA, Los Angeles*

The Smart Real Estate Investor's Guide

Your Road Map to Wealth
in *Any* Economy

Master Coach Karim Jaude
Your Partner in Real Estate

THE SMART REAL ESTATE INVESTOR'S GUIDE:
Your Road Map to Wealth in *Any* Economy

Original material Copyright 2009 by Karim Jaude
ISBN 0-9767575-8-3

Printed in the United States of America by Lightning Source, Inc.

Published by Dynamics Press
P.O. Box 491879
Los Angeles, CA 90049

First Printing

Published in the United States, Canada, and the United Kingdom

Address all queries to:
Dynamics Press
P.O. Box 491879
Los Angeles, CA 90049

This book is dedicated to my better half, Anne,
to my daughter, my son, my daughter-in-law,
and my two granddaughters
for their love, support, and inspiration.

ACKNOWLEDGEMENTS

*M*any individuals have contributed to this book. Thank you to all those who helped me.

I would like to give special thanks to my wife, Anne, and my daughter, Giselle, who helped in preparing the book. Many thanks to Eric Shaw and Joel Eisenberg for their friendship and support, to Henry (HAP) Pattiz for editing the tax chapter, to Debbie Jackson (without her this book would not have been completed), and to my assistant Lauren.

To all the people who have worked in my companies, for their loyalty and support; to all the investors who have trusted me with their money and their friendship; to all the professionals who have advised and guided me through thousands of transactions; to all my students/ mentees, for whom I lit the spark that got them into real estate investing (I learned from them as much as I taught them, and a few became even more successful than I); to all my speaker panelists and seminar attendees who kept me on my toes and pushed me to excellence—I extend my heartfelt gratitude.

CONTENTS

PART I: PREPARING YOURSELF

PART II: GETTING STARTED

PART III: PRACTICAL ASPECTS OF REAL ESTATE INVESTING

CHAPTER SIX

CREATE VALUE IN YOUR INVESTMENT PROPERTIES— IN *ANY* ECONOMY

CHAPTER SEVEN

FLIPPING THE "FIXER-UPPER"

CHAPTER EIGHT

FORECLOSURES

Part IV: TAKING YOUR SUCCESS TO THE NEXT LEVEL

CHAPTER TEN
OPM AND THE INCREDIBLE POWER OF LEVERAGE

CHAPTER THIRTEEN
TAX LIENS AND TAX DEEDS

CHAPTER FOURTEEN
YOUR KEY TO HIGHER RETURN: EFFECTIVE PROPERTY MANAGEMENT

AN UPDATE FROM THE AUTHOR

How Can *Smart Investors* Make the Best of a Real Estate Market That Has Changed Forever?

Winter 2009-2010. Early in the process of writing this book, an unprecedented event took place: Our country experienced a financial crisis of a magnitude not seen since the Great Depression. Because that crisis was caused in part by faulty real estate investments, it has changed the way real estate investors must do business. **The majority of real estate books have been written for different types of markets and teach strategies that do not work in today's challenging times.**

Here, I address the new realities of the post-subprime real estate market. The rest of my book builds upon what I discuss here and on the unchanging principles I have learned through forty-plus years of experience as a real estate investor.

—Karim Jaude

The real estate market as we knew it before 2008 has changed forever. Credit is difficult to obtain and is more expensive. Lenders have changed their rules, are underwriting more strictly and conservatively, and want to see proof of funds and prequalification before they even look at purchase offers. Appraisers are undercutting values, and tenants are becoming more educated and are demanding better service and value for their money.

Yet these changes create windows of opportunity that I haven't seen in my 45 years in the real estate business. These opportunities can be extremely lucrative for savvy investors who understand the game, play by the rules, and have the capital as well as the ability and the know-how to acquire and manage distressed properties.

Over the next eighteen months more than a *trillion* dollars of commercial real estate will be due for refinancing. Because of tighter credit, stricter underwriting, and a drop in property values of 30 to 70 percent, most of these properties will not be eligible for refinancing unless the property owners are willing and able to put more money down—creating many more opportunities for group investing.

Forty-five years ago I founded full-service real estate companies and have been operating them ever since. Many of the people who attend my real estate seminars, as well as many potential new investors, say they are interested in real estate because they have seen friends and business associates make money from the rapid appreciation of the market over the last few years, before the financial crisis. Now they want to ride the new wave of distressed properties and foreclosures the crisis has caused.

Several of them have told me they missed the wave of foreclosures in the 1990s, and they don't want to miss the current wave. Still, I urge caution when I hear the words "foreclosure" and "bargain." There are opportunities out there, but just because the property is distressed does not necessarily make it a good bargain.

Sadly, some investors are rushing to buy foreclosures without knowing what they're doing and without thoroughly performing their due diligence. Today, educating yourself about real estate investing, financing, acquisition, negotiation, and, of course, your local marketplace, is more important than ever.

In other words, real estate investors who don't want to lose their shirts must clear their minds and adapt to the new realities and opportunities of today's market.

New Market, Same Old Mistakes. Real estate investing can be an extremely lucrative as well as a risky business that requires real-life experience and practical knowledge. The mistake that many new investors fall victim to is thinking, "I need to get my first deal!" This syndrome is especially true of investors who first step into the world of real estate and see all the different options that are available. Wanting to get their feet wet in the real estate business, many new investors are willing to take just about any deal in order to feel like they are a true investor.

Making this mistake upon entering the real estate investing business could be the end of an investing career before it even begins.

Same Game, New Rules. Lenders have changed their rules and are underwriting more strictly and conservatively. However, these changes create opportunities for savvy investors who understand the game, play by the rules, and have the ability to acquire and manage distressed properties.

The Wave of the Future. In response to the realities of a changed market, most investors will turn to group investing, a.k.a. syndication, in order to raise capital. Whether it is used to refinance existing loans or to take advantage of the greatest investment opportunities that we have seen since the 1930s, syndication is the wave of the future.

The Importance of Understanding the Numbers

How to Be a Successful Real Estate Investor. In any economy, it's vitally important to be able to successfully evaluate the current market value of property based on comparables, cost of renovations, and carrying costs—after repairs are completed and enough vacancies are filled (80 percent or better) to stabilize property value. This process requires you to be able to determine the fair market value of rents as well as renovation expenses in order to complete an accurate proforma on your investment property.

Every successful investor needs to build an investment proforma for each property before considering a purchase. It is important to use a consistent methodology for all the properties you are considering so they can be compared and contrasted prior to making your investment decision.

The Vital Importance of Due Diligence. Creating a proforma means investors must complete their due diligence. Due diligence is simply the process of gathering information, verifying the data, and then processing it. The most important aspects of creating a proforma are to verify that the data you are using is accurate regarding the subject property and then to compare your information to current market data.

Verify Everything. In other words, every investor needs to corroborate via a third-party the information a seller provides. For example, if the seller states that the cost of insurance on the property is $1,600 per year, you as the investor should ask for a copy of the policy declaration and then get a comparative quote from your own insurance company. By doing that, you will have two viewpoints regarding the cost and the coverage for the expense you will incur.

It's necessary to complete the same kind of due diligence for every expense associated with a property in order to create a realistic proforma. If you don't, it's far too easy to fall into an investment that doesn't fulfill your stated objectives.

Speculation vs. Value-Added Investments

Remember all the reality shows that were on TV a while back? (*Flip This House, Flip That House*, etc.) Where did they all go? These shows disappeared in part because when the market changed it became difficult to generate a profit from flipping real estate.

Before the subprime crisis in 2008, substantial price appreciation allowed anyone who could get a mere 10 to 15 percent discount off the purchase price (minus repairs) a good chance to make a profit from an investment property. Holding costs were not a factor in the equation, because they were erased by appreciation! What that meant was the speed of rehab, the speed of finding a buyer, and the speed of closing didn't matter, as long as you had the money to pay the lender each month and pay the taxes, insurance, utilities, and maintenance.

> *Tip from the Coach:*
>
> *It is the market (and the area) that dictates the discount you'll need in order to have a fighting chance of generating a profit— not some hard and fast formula.*

Speculation in a Buyer's Market. The new reality is that we are now living in a buyer's market, and very few "speculators" (the true definition of "flippers") achieve consistent success buying houses with the intent to resell immediately. Even experienced buy-and-sell technicians have either dramatically decreased their volume or have become disenchanted and are waiting for a change in the market.

WHY?

The answer is quite simple if you've ever experienced a failed flip: Flipping properties in a buyer's market leaves NO margin for error.

Investing During a Depreciating Market. In the current soft market, property prices have been declining at a rate of 3 to 4 percent per month in some cities. When you buy an investment property to resell under those circumstances, you must buy at an even bigger discount and/or sell and close faster than during a flat or appreciating market.

For example, a basic formula for determining the strength of a deal is, after subtracting fix-up expenses, to allow 10 percent for holding costs and 10 percent for selling costs. In that case, your profit, if the full 20 percent of those costs is depleted, would be 10 percent. In other words, if you're rehabbing a $100,000 house, your profit would be $10,000. But when you figure in 3 percent for points and 1 percent per month for interest, taxes, insurance, and maintenance, *after just two months of price erosion at 3 percent per month, you've used up the 10 percent you've allocated for holding costs.*

Finding the True Rate of Appreciation

Appreciation rates for specific areas can be found through MLS (the realtors' Multiple Listing Service) data. Researching the appreciation rate on a regular basis in the areas you want to buy will give you the upper hand compared to those who always use the same old predetermined formula.

Therefore, if you don't find a qualified buyer who can close in two months, your 10 percent profit will be compromised—or eliminated altogether! But let's say you're lucky and you find a buyer and enter escrow in just a month—what if for some reason the property doesn't close? You still lose out on your profit.

These scenarios have been happening regularly throughout the country in various markets, and that is exactly why there are few rehabbers or wholesalers who are consistently flipping for profit in today's declining real estate market.

However, if you're still determined to flip real estate for profit in the current market, you would do well to keep the following in mind:

Flipping Tip #1: Getting a bigger discount off the acquisition price to compensate for price erosion costs is easier said than done, even in a buyer's market. Not to say you can't buy at below 50 percent of value, but it's much more difficult. If you make your living flipping houses, an occasional deal at a 60 to 70 percent discount won't pay the bills. Hitting singles and doubles on a consistent basis will serve you better than trying to hit a home run every time.

Flipping Tip #2: Never attempt to buy a property "all cash" with the intent to resell (wholesale or retail) unless you can buy cheaply enough and employ the right exit strategy. (In this case, the cash to buy comes from your bank account, a loan, or an equity-sharing agreement under which another speculator puts up the cash to "buy and fix" for a chance to earn a percentage of the profit. The cash at closing comes from either a cash buyer or a buyer who obtains a loan.)

Flipping Tip #3: It doesn't make financial sense to convert a property that was bought to flip into a rental property if you borrowed short-term with hard or private money. Your strategy should be (unless you decide to refinance with long-term money) to sell at a discount, learn from your experience, and either wait until the market picks up or figure out a better strategy to flip properties while prices are declining.

Flipping Tip #4: Why do we invest? To generate a profit. That can be done by flipping properties, buying short sales, and buying foreclosures, but real estate investing is most profitable in markets where there is job creation and inward migration (people moving into urban areas). Inward migration is better both for finding renters and for finding buyers.

However, always keep in mind that it is substantially easier to make a profit in an appreciating market, or even in a flat market.

Jerry bought two houses in foreclosure in San Diego County. He put down 25 percent and obtained hard money loans at 12 percent for 75 percent of the purchase price, or 60 percent of the future value of the houses. For several months Jerry was not able to flip or rent the houses and lost them to the hard money lenders. Of course, not only did he lose his money, he ruined his credit as well.

Finding Investment Information via the Internet

Globalization is no longer science fiction; it's real. The world is getting smaller, and computers make it even smaller. The Internet can bring the entire real estate market to your fingertips. Live where you want to live, but invest only where it makes financial sense. With the Internet, it's easy to find out where the opportunities are.

Investing During a Neutral Market. Even in a neutral market, that is, one in which prices are relatively flat, as a property rehabber you must fix, sell, and close faster than in an appreciating market in order to have a chance of making a profit. Holding costs are definitely a factor in a "flat" market. Failure to get the property sold and closed in four to six months can significantly affect your bottom line, which is very different than in an appreciating market where there is no deadline.

Investing During an Appreciating Market. In an appreciating market you can pay more for a property than in a neutral or a soft market. Yet each area of a given city is different, so it's important to do your research, a.k.a. due diligence. Some areas will appreciate more than others, and inventory levels will be different from place to place. These factors can affect the length of time it takes to find a qualified buyer who wants to purchase your property.

However, even in the prior appreciating market, I personally adhered to the standard of acquiring a property at a 30 percent discount, minus repairs, before I would buy. Consequently, I didn't buy as many properties to flip for profit as I could have. Instead, I concentrated on mid- to long-term investments in value-added properties.

The Power of Cash

Buying real estate solely for flipping is often a big gamble in today's market. But if you buy real estate to hold for five to ten years or longer, you'll most likely make *a lot* of money.

If you buy a distressed property at a big discount and flip it within a year, you *might* be able to make some money. But if you are not able to flip that property and you want to rent it instead, you need to rent it within a few months (preferably within a few weeks).

Yet even if your investment property produces cash flow from day one, you should also have enough cash reserves to carry the property if the tenant doesn't pay or moves out.

The Importance of Cash Flow. Those who have attended my Smart Real Estate Investors Seminars have heard me say again and again, "The two most important words in real estate investing are CASH FLOW." Of course, we don't make big money from cash flow alone, but cash flow is necessary to help carry the property during hard times. When the market picks up (and it almost always picks up and even surpasses the peak level of the previous market), then your *real* money is made from appreciation.

My gardener in Los Angeles, Lupe, bought five distressed homes in San Antonio on eBay and moved there to fix and rent them.

One of my students, Gordon, who lives in Santa Barbara, used the Internet to buy an apartment building in Colorado Springs.

Another student of mine, Phillip, lives in Paris and bought a shopping center in Austin, Texas, also using the Internet.

The Importance of Cash Reserves. When you invest, it is imperative to keep enough cash reserves on hand. The amount of cash reserves you need depends on the location, the type of property, the age and condition of the property, and the market in the area. In other words, in order to stay in real estate for the long term, you need cash reserves.

Lack of cash flow or cash reserves puts unnecessary pressure on you to do substandard repairs, accept less than qualified tenants, and sell under pressure.

What Having the Right Information Can Do for You

Investing in real estate is a lot like surfing—if you don't catch the wave at the right time with the right information, you'll get toppled over.

My hope is that you will closely analyze the market and the area in which you're buying *each time* you purchase a house, apartment building, or commercial property and then calculate the price that will give you the best chance of generating a profit. Lastly, you must also determine the appropriate exit strategy that has the best chance of accomplishing your investment goals.

In the pages ahead, you'll discover that we make most of our money in real estate when *buying*. That is, if you buy right and don't have to sell, you'll always make money in real estate.

It's having the right information at the right time that will help you do just that—be able to buy right and then become, as I have done, a successful real estate investor.

All the best,

Master Coach Karim Jaude
Your Partner in Real Estate

Tip from the Coach:

Buying real estate with nothing down is easy; handling negative cash flow, repairs, and other expenses in the meantime is the challenge.

PREFACE

*B*y the age of twenty-six, Karim Jaude (pronounced "Ka-reem Jow-dee") had earned his first $1 million buying and rehabbing distressed properties and businesses. This is all the more impressive when one considers that Karim, a native of Lebanon, came to America from Iran—disguised as a woman—after escaping from a series of terrorist plots and kidnappings. In fact, it is the discipline bred of Karim's unique personal travails that has led directly to his continuing good fortune.

Karim founded and operated nineteen successful companies in eight countries. To date, his offices have handled more than $20 billion in real estate transactions.

Karim has developed, invested in, rehabbed, financed, and managed properties ranging from single family homes to condo projects and apartment buildings, from shopping centers to office and industrial buildings . . . from hotels to land to mixed-use properties.

In other words, *The Smart Real Estate Investor's Guide* is no primer written by an inexperienced theorist. It is, in essence, a bible of cumulative experience written by an individual who faced both the highs and lows of the real estate market and yet always managed ultimately to come out on top.

The book is peppered with fascinating real-life stories of property owners, buyers, sellers, managers, and investors, many who worked with Karim. And he tells it like is—both the good and the bad.

For the past forty years, Karim has committed and never failed to help at least one person every single day. This is how he lives his life; this also explains the popularity of his standing-room-only monthly Smart Real Estate Investors Seminars held in Los Angeles for the last eight years. In January 2009 he also began hosting real estate seminars in Orange County, California.

Karim also acts as a coach and mentor to a small number of students who dream of replicating his success . . . which is why he wants to pass along his knowledge to you right here and now. He would like anyone who reads this book to be able to use it as a *Road Map to Success in* Any *Economy*.

To do just that, refer to this book on a regular basis—and may your holdings thrive!

FOREWORD

I have known Karim Jaude for twenty years. And what a twenty years it has been!

What I have learned from this guy!

My name is Eric Shaw; I run a professional networking organization called the All Cities Network. Within our network we have bankers and lenders as members, media professionals, attorneys, accountants, and now, real estate professionals. Prior to the recent formation of our real estate group, I disallowed—for various reasons—real estate professionals into my network. Except for Karim Jaude.

In my capacity as a professional networker, I have rarely, okay, I have *never* come across someone as well-liked and reliable as Karim. He is an expert, an educator, and a true friend. If anyone I know has a question about real estate, I send them to Karim. Why? Because the way we do anything, is the way we do everything. That is among the prime lessons in my own teachings, and Karim has always served to help and inspire his fellow man.

He lives his philosophy—help one person every single day, and you will be rewarded with a life of unaccountable riches.

Karim is from Lebanon and has done business in Iran; I only mention this as he is something of a colorful character—he once disguised himself as a woman to escape the country when revolution erupted in Iran. He is also free with his advice and is a true leader.

I highly recommend Karim's book. In fact, I cannot recommend it highly enough. Within these pages both the novice and seasoned investor will find valuable wisdom to succeed in both the real estate life and in the real world.

You are in for a treat . . .

Eric Shaw
The All Cities Network
www.allcities.org

INTRODUCTION

O n a beautiful winter evening some thirty years ago, I arrived in Los Angeles with no money, no friends, and without a strong command of the English language. I came from Lebanon, by way of Iran, with only $17 in my pocket and my American Express card.

The mission of this book is to help you do even better in real estate than I have done.

Just a few short years later, I had built a full-service real estate company and a successful business-coaching/mentoring practice. So how did a foreigner with the most rudimentary English skills and no net worth to speak of become a highly successful earner seemingly overnight? My fundamental method was simple: I started investing in houses. Though I knew nothing about the L.A. housing market—or the U.S. housing market for that matter—I followed my fundamental method and targeted middle- to low-income areas near where I wanted to live. These areas were Mar Vista, Venice, Culver City, and Westchester in West Los Angeles. In a few weeks I made more than thirty offers on every house in the market, plus half a dozen homes that were not yet listed.

The first two real estate agents I worked with told me I was not realistic and gave up (too) early on me. The third real estate agent, however, was so impressed with my panache that he chose to invest his own money with me. Then . . . so did my lawyer, and one of his friends. We bought the first house in Mar Vista, fixed it up, and sold it within three months. With the profits we bought three more houses . . .

and the rest is history. The bottom line is that to this day I continue to make offers, and I continue to make money.

Now I purchase mostly larger properties.

> *Tip from the Coach:*
>
> *The secret of investing in real estate is to invest in real estate.*

If I could do that up against every challenge imaginable, then each and every one of you can do it too.

First, you must have a *clear vision* of exactly what it is that you want to achieve. Second, set and write down your goals, make a plan to achieve them, and be willing to pay the price and make the necessary sacrifices. Make certain you get focused, and then get yourself out there.

I knew what I wanted, and I would stop at nothing to attain it within legal and moral guidelines. I also understood early on that everything has a price and that there are few shortcuts to success. It's simple. If you are determined, you will win most of the time. If you are not, you won't.

People tend to respond when their efforts begin to pay off. These efforts in turn motivate further effort, producing even further results. In my experience, the quickest way to achieve your goals is to develop strong time management skills. Statistics show that most of us waste 20 to 80 percent of our time on unproductive tasks. Now, consider spending that misemployed time on opportunistic endeavors, and imagine what you can achieve.

The secret of investing in real estate is to invest in real estate. You might ask, "Karim, what kind of advice is that?" My answer to that question is once again: *The secret to investing in real estate is to invest in real estate.* What gives?

The biggest problem most people have is that they wait. That's all. To those people, I say, "Don't wait! Do it, and *then* wait." The biggest mistake you can make is doing nothing. That leads to a lack of motivation, which leads to a lack of determination, which leads to . . . nothing. Invest while you are learning about the business, don't wait until you learn everything before you start investing.

Remember: Good ideas alone do not lead to success, but good ideas with immediate action will.

Robin has been married for five years. She has been to half a dozen seminars about investing in real estate and read several books, but never invested in real estate or bought any properties. She does not have the time or the money. She doesn't know where to start. She's afraid to make a mistake: pay too much, buy the wrong property in the wrong area, etc. She just can't make a decision.

Please put your excuses to the side if I'm going to be your teacher and this book is going to be your guide. If you want to buy a home or investment property but lack the adequate funds for a down payment or closing costs, do you just forget it? After all, that's probably the most common response you will get from people who think they know what they are talking about. You must forget that kind of thinking right now; those people are wrong. I refused to think that way, and look what happened.

You certainly *can* make money purchasing properties with no money down; you just have to develop a fastidious selection process. Often there is a reason why properties are available for no money down, and you don't want somebody else's problem to become yours. But as long as you make certain that your investment is sound, you will absolutely profit from it.

Again, it's important to first define your objectives. Are you buying a house, condo, or a townhouse to live in? Are you buying one-to-four residential units as an investment, perhaps planning to live in one and rent the others? Or are you buying a property solely as an investment; concentrating on apartments, commercial units, mixed-use buildings, etc.? If so, do you want to flip it (selling it as soon as possible) or do you want to keep it for the long term for cash flow and appreciation?

I have made fortunes in real estate, and I have made my share of mistakes. And that means several times I have lost my shirt.

And let me tell you there is no joy in the loss. There are, however, numerous lessons I have learned as a result of those, in hindsight, valuable times.

> *I have made fortunes in real estate and I've lost my shirt a few times. The goal of this book is to help you minimize your mistakes and to help you keep your shirt!*

My mission today is to help you to do even better than I have done. I want you to benefit from my experience and reduce your mistakes, so you can make your fortune and keep your shirt.

I am happy to say that nowadays I'm never anything less than fully clothed.

The lessons I will be sharing with you in these pages are gathered from my years of experience and will enable you to become the best real estate investor you can possibly be.

In that spirit, let's begin.

Master Coach Karim Jaude
Your Partner in Real Estate

PART I:
PREPARING YOURSELF

CHAPTER ONE

WHY REAL ESTATE IS THE "IDEAL" INVESTMENT—IN ANY ECONOMY

*S*tatistics show that 71 percent of millionaires in this country have made their fortunes in real estate. That reason alone is the best response to the question: *Why real estate?* In fact, real estate is the IDEAL investment. Take a look at the following acronym:

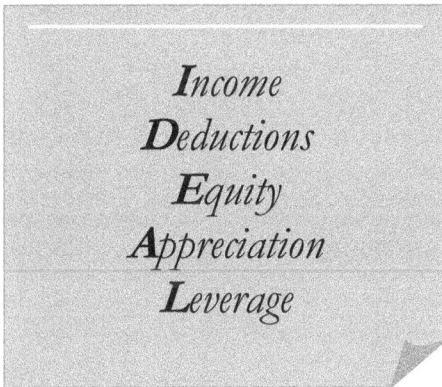

Income
Deductions
Equity
Appreciation
Leverage

Your **IDEAL** investment allows you to produce Income, maximize Deductions, build Equity, provides room for Appreciation, and optimizes your ability to Leverage your property. Those IDEALs are what make real estate your best bet for steady financial growth.

Income

The most important benefit of real estate investing is income, specifically net cash income. What is "net cash income"? It's the remaining cash in hand after you've paid your operating expenses and the mortgage payments on your property (see Figure 1). It's also called "positive cash flow." Put simply, it's the money that stays in your pocket each month.

Figure 1

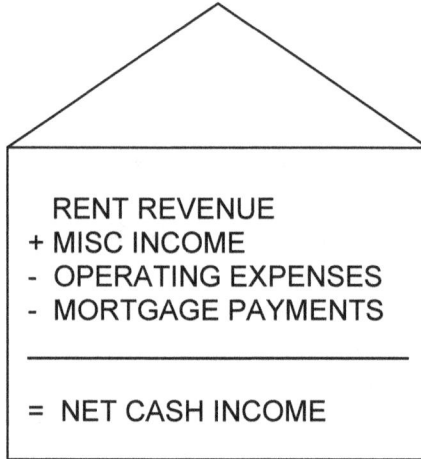

RENT REVENUE
+ MISC INCOME
- OPERATING EXPENSES
- MORTGAGE PAYMENTS
_____

= NET CASH INCOME

Deductions

Another major benefit of investing in real estate is that the U.S. government allows you to deduct certain expenses, namely interest and depreciation, from your revenues as you compute the "taxable income" amount from your investment property (see Figure 2).

Figure 2

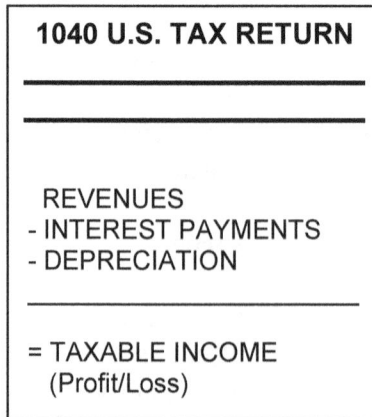

1040 U.S. TAX RETURN
_____
_____

REVENUES
- INTEREST PAYMENTS
- DEPRECIATION
_____

= TAXABLE INCOME
(Profit/Loss)

Therefore, since you pay tax on your profit (taxable income), not on the gross (cash) income from your real estate business endeavor, you can own a property with a substantial cash income that produces no taxable profit. In fact, the *smart real estate investor* might have cash income, but show a loss on paper. That loss, in turn, may be deducted from your profits from other properties or other sources of taxable income, depending on the tax regulations that apply to your situation (be sure to get advice from a reputable tax professional).

In reality, depreciation deductions are artificial amounts created by the government. A property that is well located and aggressively managed and maintained does *not* depreciate, and for that reason most countries around the world do not allow tax deductions for depreciation on real estate.

Keep in mind that allowable tax deductions can and do change at the whim of the government. Real estate deductions were affected by the 1986-87 tax reforms, for example. For the time being, however, deductions are still very much a reward for investing in real estate.

Of course, the *smart real estate investor* never lets these tax shelters be the prime reason for investing. Instead, look at them as the icing on the investment "profit" cake.

Equity

Equity buildup occurs when your tenants are making payments that you use to pay the mortgage on your property. Since in most cases part of your mortgage payment includes an amount applied to principal (or equity), your tenants are paying for your growing percentage of ownership in the property.

Philip, one of many people I have coached, liked to purchase properties in St Louis, Missouri, with a 20 percent down payment. He paid his mortgages off within fifteen years. We figured that if the real estate market stayed flat for fifteen years, his capital would increase four times. In addition, he would also have both the tax benefits and cash flow.

The *smart real estate investor* knows that equity buildup due to loan amortization is realistic as long as the property was purchased at a price within the comparable market norm, or at less than market value. Property market values also must be maintaining or growing in order for equity to grow.

Appreciation

Appreciation is the growth in value of a property. Value can go up because of inflation, i.e., a rise in the cost of living, as well as increased market demand—or may occur because you have done something to the property to create additional value, such as improving curb appeal or installing upgrades. Appreciation is the prime reason people choose to own income property, because the rewards can be substantial.

As with equity buildup, the *smart real estate investor* knows that appreciation is more likely when a property has been purchased at or below market value and then aggressively and efficiently managed.

Figure 3

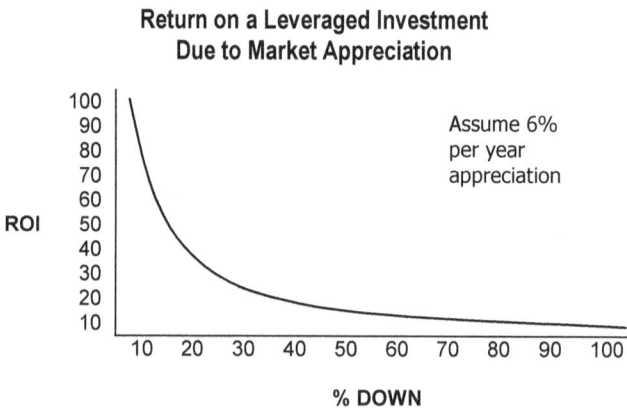

Return on a Leveraged Investment Due to Market Appreciation

Leverage

Leverage is the result of borrowing purchase monies in order to multiply the return. Figure 3 shows a curve on a graph indicating the "return on investment" (ROI) when a property is leveraged at various levels (a property value appreciation of 6 percent per year is assumed). As shown, with a property leveraged at 75 percent (i.e., using a 25 percent down payment), the return on investment per year is 20 percent.

Generally speaking, the higher the leverage, the higher the ROI. There is, however, a catch: *Higher leverage equals higher mortgage payments*. The result is that the more the property is leveraged, the greater the risk for negative cash flow (cash coming out of your pocket each month to keep and maintain the property). That, in turn, means a greater risk of losing the project and your investment entirely.

Consequently, the *smart real estate investor* uses leverage prudently and in concert with the other IDEAL rewards of real estate in order to produce the highest return on investment that can comfortably be obtained. The term "calculated risk" applies here, because the risk absolutely should be carefully considered. The *smart real estate investor* usually finds that a 60 to 80 percent leverage (a 20 to 40 percent down payment) is a prudent decision. How *much* leverage depends on the type of property, its location, the market, and your tolerance for risk.

The bottom line? A *smart real estate investor* can use the five principle IDEALs—Income, Deductions, Equity, Appreciation, and Leverage—as a rewards system to build wealth.

The Three Most Important Real Estate Myths Debunked

In addition to the five positive IDEALs that make up an effective system of rewards for the *smart real estate investor*, I have discovered over my forty-plus years of experience in real estate that there are three dangerous myths that cause people either to make bad investment decisions or to avoid investing in real estate entirely:

Myth #1: "All you need is cash flow." If you think you can become wealthy in real estate with cash flow only, you're wrong. You might as well be straightening deck chairs on the Titanic. It's simply not going to happen. The way you become wealthy in real estate is through *appreciation*.

You can become wealth*ier* with cash flow, but only after you've already obtained a certain level of wealth. If you're thinking about investing in rental properties, a prime producer of cash flow, you should also first have some degree of certainty (or at least a good estimate) of how those rental properties will appreciate.

Hans liked to purchase properties for all cash. He built a small fortune. However, he could have purchased many more properties and his fortune could have been much bigger if he had acquired loans.

Myth #2: "There are no more tax benefits." In fact, tax benefits are the second most important reason why people invest in real estate. The most important reason is to make money.

Tax benefits mean that the government is paying for part of your investment. The return on your investment, after taxes, is much greater because of the tax benefits of real estate investing. Furthermore, additional tax benefits can be derived by exchanging your way to tax-free wealth by using 1031 tax deferred exchanges (read more about 1031s in Chapter Twelve).

Yvonne has been building a fortune in real estate without paying a dime in income tax. She found a way to shelter her cash flow through depreciation and cost segregation and increased her capital through 1031 exchanges.

Myth #3: "Location = locale." You have repeatedly heard the term "location, location, location" regarding purchasing property . . . and location *is* very important. But too many investors confuse *location* with *locale*. That is, investors tend to look at rental properties within a short driving distance of where they live, but if there are no opportunities for appreciation in those areas, you should not be looking locally. You should look for pockets of opportunity—no matter where they might exist. In this book we will show you not only *where* to buy real estate investments, but also *how* to determine *when* to make your purchase (read more in Chapters Three, Four, and Five).

In 2003 the real estate market became so heated in California, I started buying properties in Arizona and Nevada instead. In February 2006 I sold my properties in Arizona and Nevada and started buying in Texas and Colorado. After the subprime crisis in 2007-08 caused real estate prices to tumble, I once again began making most of my purchases in California.

Finally, never forget that investing in real estate is hard work. Although profits can be spectacular, there is no legal and easy "get-rich-quick" scheme that works, either for the beginner or for the savvy investor. There are, however, legitimate real estate investment techniques that work. If you master them and take proper action, you'll be ahead of the game and have a better shot at success.

> ### Tip from the Coach:
>
> **Although real estate profits can be spectacular, there is no easy "get-rich-quick" scheme that works. But if you master legitimate techniques—and take proper action— you'll be ahead of the game and have a better shot at success.**

It's also important to remain realistic, because along with the rewards come the pitfalls. Sometimes it's the hassle of always having to deal with tenants, neighbors, agencies, or lenders. Sometimes it's the tediousness and red tape of wading through local and state laws. You also must remember (as is true for any other segment of the economy) that real estate has its own cycles. For example, if liquidity isn't readily available in the marketplace, you may not be able to get the financing you need. All these factors can result in huge headaches.

Yet real estate investing is currently attracting more amateur and professional investors than any other field. As we told you at the beginning of the chapter, *most* private fortunes in this country have been made in real estate.

Even though the industry can be a tough place for an amateur, it can also be fun and creative. Deals are being made every day, even during hard times. (Perhaps the *real* deals happen during the toughest times!)

I believe there are great days coming for those who can first see and then seize the opportunities available in real estate. But without doubt, to make it in this business you must remain *focused* and *dedicated*!

CHAPTER TWO

IS REAL ESTATE FOR *YOU?*

*T*he first question all potential real estate investors should ask themselves is: *Is real estate for me?* To help answer that question, when I am coaching my clients I teach them "Karim's foolproof formula to success in business and real estate":

> ### Tip from the Coach:
>
> 1. ***You must love what you do.***
> 2. ***It must have the potential to make money.***
> 3. ***If you love something that doesn't have the potential to make money—***
>   **love something else!**

Mind-set is the most important factor in real estate investment. A real estate investor *must* have the belief, the desire, and the determination in order to succeed. You must love what you do, or you won't keep up the level of motivation and discipline necessary for success.

"But," you say, "I want to buy a home or investment property, and I don't have money for a down payment or closing costs."

"Well, just forget it." That's probably what you've been told by people who think they know what they are talking about—but they don't! If you have the correct mental approach, but lack funds, there are always ways to develop capital. In other words, if you have the desire and determination, the know-how and the money will follow.

Bob and Margie had been married for five years. They wanted to start a family. Margie wanted to stay at home, but they couldn't afford to do so. Bob was good with his hands, and Margie was a good manager and bookkeeper. I helped them buy (and manage) an apartment building so that Margie could work from home.

First, you must understand your own purpose and motivation. What makes you tick? Not every investment or business opportunity is the best course of action for everyone. We're all different and respond to different circumstances accordingly. You must choose a vocation that you enjoy and are enthusiastic about, an arena in which you have a comfort level that then enables you to achieve your personal goals and business objectives.

Tip from the Coach:

What does it take to build a fortune in today's tough real estate market? The same principles that have always been required:

- ❖ *Vision*—you must know exactly what you want.
- ❖ A *Commitment* to learn the principles of smart real estate investing.
- ❖ The *Discipline* to stay focused and to follow principles—rather than your ego or emotions.
- ❖ A *Business Plan* that holds up in both good and bad times.

Once you know you have the correct mind-set, then you're ready to follow four essential principles required for any *smart investor* to build wealth in any real estate market.

Vision: The First Step to Making Your First Million

In my forty years in the real estate business, I have met thousands of real estate investors with many different levels of knowledge and experience. Some have become amazingly successful, some did reasonably well, and others have experienced dramatic failure. In the last twenty years, I have helped eighteen people become millionaires. One of them was working for me as a gardener. Another person worked for me as a handyman. Without a doubt, there is money to be made in real estate if you do your homework and are willing to do what it takes.

Successful real estate investors I have known include:

❖ Ph.D.s
❖ High school dropouts
❖ Men and women of all races and backgrounds
❖ People born in poverty
❖ Heirs/heiresses born with silver spoons in their mouths
❖ People who have started from scratch

They all have one thing in common. They all knew exactly what they wanted.

More than a hundred years ago Mark Twain said, "I can teach anybody how to get what they want out of life. The problem is I can't find anybody who can tell me what they want." Ask yourself: Do you really know what you want? Are you sure? If not . . . take the time to find out!

The first step is to have a clear *vision*; know exactly what you want for yourself and your business. Then, set specific goals and create a detailed plan for how to achieve them:

❖ What do you want to achieve in ten, twenty, or thirty years?
❖ What will you be doing then?
❖ Where would you like to be living?
❖ How much will your net worth be?

I often think of a scene from Alice's Adventures in Wonder-land, *when Alice came to a fork in the road and saw a Cheshire cat in a tree. "Which road do I take?" she asked. "Where do you want to go?" was his response. "I don't know," Alice answered. "Then," said the cat, "it doesn't matter which way you go."*

I would add: If you don't know where you're going, you'll never know when you get there.

When Texas billionaire H. L. Hunt, who made his fortune in real estate, was asked the secret to his success, he responded, "Success requires two things. You must know exactly what you want, and you must set goals. Make a plan to achieve them and be willing to pay the price. Then focus and get busy paying that price."

Once you have a clear vision, you must set specific and measurable goals. Then create a daily plan for how to achieve them.

Why Goal Setting is Important

In a survey of millionaires, when asked the single most important skill that led to their success, 93 percent of the respondents said "setting and writing down specific and measurable goals." Setting goals (and *writing them down*) is imperative, not only because it is a motivating factor, but because they act as markers, enabling you to recognize what works and what doesn't on your pathway forward.

Furthermore, your goals must be your own; they must belong to you, and only to you. I like to think of goals as guilt-free dreams and aspirations inspired by what you truly desire, not what someone else (or society) expects from you or what you feel pressured into from misplaced guilt. The weight-loss goals many people set are a perfect example of this mistaken kind of inspiration. Planning to shed pounds to make your partner happy is a sure path to defeat and depression. The weight you lose for someone else never stays off—because you didn't do it for yourself. Your goals must be your own, and they must inspire *you*.

> *We don't have to know how to achieve our goals; we just have to want to achieve them. A lot of people fail to achieve their goals in life because they tell themselves they don't know how. This is just an excuse for inaction. The truth is, when we focus on what we want with passion, the way to get there becomes evident.*
>
> —*Kevin Lawrence, business coach*

Select just a few goals—but make them invigorating. Limit yourself to seven short-term goals. You can have as many long-term goals as you want.

Long-term goals can be extravagant and imaginative; go ahead, really stretch the boundaries of plausibility and think of what you truly desire! Large, inspiring goals put your subconscious mind to work creating paths for achievement.

Setting big, inspiring goals can be a scary matter, but skip the how to . . . for now! Just set goals. Your goals should always inspire you, and help to measure your success; I always like to know where I am in relationship to my goals.

Your goals should be clear, specific, and measurable. When you set short-term goals, choose steps that will help you reach the larger goals. The more specific your goals, the more focused your mind becomes.

Zig Ziglar, arguably the greatest motivational speaker of our time, asks his audiences a question you might well ask yourself; "Do you want to be a meaningful specific, or a wandering generality?"

When you set a goal, be certain how to answer these three questions: Do I really want this goal? How badly do I want it? Am I willing to do what it takes to achieve it?

Then, *reveal* your goals. That's right. Tell people what your goals are and ask for help in reaching them. Successful people enjoy helping others reach success. You never know who and why someone might help you. Plus, telling others about your goals creates a compelling motivation toward action. You will feel accountable, which will propel you forward to take the necessary steps toward achieving your goals.

When I was in high school, my goal was to enroll at the University Libre in Brussels, Belgium. I had very good grades, but was accepted only under the condition that I could prove my financial ability to pay the full tuition. I was working and studying at the time and was unable to provide this proof. I refused to give up so easily. I discussed the issue with several of my friends, seeking support and ideas regarding this particular roadblock.

As it turned out, one of them knew the Lebanese ambassador to Belgium. Through that connection I was able to schedule a meeting. I put together a proposal and met with the ambassador at his house for one hour. I provided him with proof of my academic abilities, the manner in which I had been paying my tuition so far, and the ULB application and letter of acceptance form listing the conditions. Three months later I was accepted to ULB due to my tenacity and the influence of the friendly ambassador. That achievement was possible because I had a deep desire and a specific goal.

But—only tell the positive people in your life your goals. You can't and shouldn't share all of your goals with everyone.

Remember: When you hit a milestone along the way, *reward yourself* for achieving that goal. Plan each milestone, and your reward will help keep you focused.

Finally, identifying your life's values is also a very important factor in achieving your dreams. There is no satisfaction in meeting a goal if it means you have bent or broken a life value to achieve it. When your acts fall out of sync with your beliefs, you throw yourself off balance. You may well feel moral angst and discomfort in the victory, which robs you of the joy *and* the victory.

Make a Commitment to Learn

Once you're sure your mind-set is correct and that you have a vision and goals, you can begin to think about the practical aspects of real estate investment.

The second step, then, is to work on yourself—your personal development and skills: the specifics of real estate investment plus communication, organization, discipline, negotiation, time management, and decision making. (Yes, you can learn how to make quick decisions so that you don't lose great opportunities simply because you were unable to make your due diligence fast enough.)

More than fifty years ago Earl Nightingale, the father of motivational speakers, said, "If you learn about any subject one hour a day, read, listen to tapes, or attend workshops and seminars, you will become expert in five years or less." He added that you must learn about the following:

- ❖ Learn as much you can about all the aspects of your business or job.
- ❖ Learn as much as you can about your chosen industry.
- ❖ Learn as much as you can about people, what motivates them, and how to communicate with them.

I strongly recommend that you work with another person: your significant other, a member of your family, a friend, a colleague, a partner. Find someone who will complement your strengths and weaknesses. In my experience, those who work together as a team achieve much better results much faster.

> *Anything we persist in doing becomes easier to do, not because the nature of the thing has changed, but because our ability grew.*
>
> *—Lynda J. Jones*

You also must learn good time management; 80 percent of people waste a large percentage of their time on all the unproductive things they do. Don't fall into that trap.

One way to effectively manage your time is to write down your

tasks for the next day before you go to bed every night. Make a list of
what needs to be done and divide it into three categories:

❖ First: "Things that must be done." These are tasks you must
  accomplish. You start your day doing what you have to do until
  you've checked off all items on that list. Don't jump ahead.
❖ Second: "Things I'd like to do." You do those tasks only after
  completing those on your must-do list.
❖ Third: "Things I would like to do if I had the time." Those tasks
  are least important; you keep them for last.

*Philip, a financial planner, did everything himself from licking
stamps to developing a strategic plan. He was burned out,
frustrated, and only marginally successful. He came to me for help. I
encouraged him to hire an assistant and focus on the important
things in his business so he could spend most of his time with his
clients or potential clients. Philip was able to reduce his workload by
two hours every day and triple his income in two years. He didn't
just take action, he took* proper *action.*

It also helps if you are a morning person. Start early in the morning
as you battle the most difficult tasks that really must be done. But if
you are an afternoon/evening person, like several of my employees,
you *can* adapt, if you are disciplined. My nephew, for example, comes
to work at 3:00 P.M. and likes to work through the night.

Remember the old adage that applies to any long-term project or
large task? *How do you eat an elephant? One bite at a time.* But to eat
an entire elephant, you must keep biting the elephant.

Next, you must learn to be a good manager. In his commencement
speech at my university graduation, the dean of the business school told
us there are no good and bad businesses, just good and bad management. In real estate, I also believe there are no good or bad markets, just
good and bad deals. I have seen bad deals in good markets, and I've
seen profitable deals made in the so-called worst markets. You must
learn to recognize the difference.

Over the years I have learned that we make most of our money by buying right. If we don't *have* to buy, and if we don't *have* to sell, we can always make money in real estate. Moreover, if you buy the right property and create value, rather than just depending on the market, you will always find opportunities.

Sometimes favorable circumstances are everywhere and prospects seemingly around every corner. And sometimes it's the exact opposite. But if you do your homework, learn to make *smart* choices, and remain vigilant, opportunities will always emerge.

> ### *Tip from the Coach:*
>
> ***You will make most of your money by buying right.***
> ***If you don't have to buy, and if you don't have to sell, you can always make money in real estate.***

Remember: There is no sure way to make a lot of money quickly in real estate, but the path is open and the opportunities are golden.

You'll make deals and discover the excitement and self-respect of handling real estate. Don't expect miracles or instant riches, but do seek the challenge of making money in creative ways. Winning in real estate is just a matter of knowing how to learn through trial and error. And if you want to reduce your mistakes, seek professional advice.

This book was meant to keep you out of trouble. It will also make you aware of the vast opportunities and risks in the rapidly changing world of real estate.

You'll learn how to be responsible for the success and failure of your real estate investments. You'll learn to understand your own motivations and that you must select the real estate opportunities that fit your character, interests, and means.

There are great opportunities in real estate, and new fortunes will continue to be created from those opportunities. More importantly, many smaller fortunes can be made, but only when investors understand what they are doing and why, when they seek advice, when they know the marketplace, and when they carefully watch their investments—and because they take nothing for granted.

This book will help you develop the knowledge you need to understand what real estate is all about. And it will help you develop a real estate investment strategy that is both financially and emotionally rewarding.

Be Disciplined

To create success and live your dream is to be disciplined. Don't let the appetite of the moment steal your chance of future success. No one can be motivated all the time, but if you are disciplined, you will stay focused and do what you have to do when it needs to be done.

Compare discipline to changing a baby's diaper. It needs to be done when it needs to be done, whether you like it or not, and you must do it thoroughly. Given the choice of staffing my team with disciplined people or motivated people, I choose the disciplined person every time.

Additionally, keep in mind that no matter what type of real estate investment you choose, you must realize that you are operating a *business* and it must be treated as a business. If you treat real estate investment like a hobby, you will get hobby results.

Further, you must form an LLC, or any other necessary entities, to protect your other assets. You never know what could happen, and you never know who might sue you for what. Be cautious and alert. Then, open a bank account, keep your business accounts separate, and do not mix business finances in with your personal accounts.

As with any aspect of life, your effort, commitment, and persistence in the real estate business will ensure long-term success. To succeed takes both focus and discipline.

Create a Business Plan

To run your real estate investment business effectively, you need a business plan. Remember: Lenders use your business plan to measure the stability and potential of your business, so your business plan should be professionally done.

Make sure your business plan is confident and optimistic, but not overly idealistic. Don't gloss over possible problems or risks. Be detailed about your plans for the future, don't overlook contingencies, and discuss your management team's strengths and skills set, even if at first the "team" is just you.

Be sure to include the goals you have set for your real estate investing business. In your business plan, answer the same kinds of questions you asked yourself when you were deciding whether or not real estate investment was for you:

- What are your objectives?
- What types of properties will you focus on purchasing? (Foreclosures? Short sales? Bank-owned?)
- Where will these properties be located?
- What price range are you considering?
- How will you finance each property?
- Will you get a bank loan? What kind?
- Will you invest the equity in your own home?
- Will you solicit investors?
- Will you have a partner? Will you use cash?

There are many online and community resources that offer help with writing a professional business plan, including the Small Business Administration (SBA) at www.sba.gov.

Karim's Twelve Most Powerful Investment Ideas

In summary, here are the twelve most powerful ideas I have used in my own life on the way to continued success in real estate investing:

1. Define your vision. Make sure you know exactly what you really want. You must be clear and specific.
2. Set as many long-term goals as you want. Some of them may be huge. But set only three to seven short-term goals. Use your short-term goals to help you achieve the long-term ones.
3. Take six steps/actions every day toward reaching your goals. The top six things on your daily action list should focus on your goals. Otherwise, you fall victim to the tyranny of the urgent.
4. Make plans and take *proper* actions, not just any actions.
5. Be self-disciplined.
6. Place a placard in plain view of your work area that reads, "Is

this the best use of my time right now? Will it help me reach my goals?" Discipline yourself to comply with it.

7. Whatever tasks you begin, finish. A path scattered with unfinished tasks takes you off your focus—fast!
8. Be on time.
9. Live in the moment and stay focused.
10. Make promises thoughtfully. Then do what you promised you would do.
11. Be persistent.
12. Reward yourself and celebrate each success.

Remember: I have built nineteen successful companies on three continents. The *one* constant from place to place has been that I have set specific goals and worked toward achieving them.

> ### *Tip from the Coach:*
>
> *The fastest way to earn your first $1 million is to know what you want, have a plan, and be willing to pay the price.*

PART II:
GETTING STARTED

CHAPTER THREE

COMMERCIAL vs. RESIDENTIAL

*W*hether you choose to invest in commercial or residential properties (or, eventually, both) will be determined by what you want and where you see yourself in the future *and* by asking yourself the following questions: In what areas do I want to invest? With what types of property do I feel comfortable? Do I want to buy fixer-uppers and sell? Or do I want to hold properties for cash flow and appreciation?

I came to Los Angeles in 1979 with $17 in my pocket. For a few months, I focused on single family homes, because that was the only option I had (and the easiest) and because I needed cash flow to live on. At that time, the cycle was at its end, and prices were starting to drop, so I had to make almost forty offers to buy one house at a good price. (I believed then as I do now: There is always a high demand for housing and plenty of opportunities for investment, even in a slow market.) A few months later, I started buying apartments. Then I branched out into retail, two years later into industrial, and then into offices. I only branched out after each division of my company was well structured and I had a team in place to take care of the existing properties.

Once you do make a decision, stick with it for a while. Get to know a particular area and type of property very well. Become an expert in that market. The more you focus on one area and type, the less you'll become frustrated, and the quicker you'll make your millions. Don't let the temptation of a deal here and a deal there divert you from your objectives. After you have experienced success in a certain niche, once you have a team in place, and once your business is well structured, then you can think of diversification.

The Benefits and Disadvantages of Each Property Type

Choosing the type of property to invest in is crucial. Each kind of property has its own cycle as well as its own temptations and pitfalls. Each type of property fulfills a different need. I started with single family homes and quickly moved to apartments because each met a different need. Some properties offer cash flow, some offer appreciation, others offer tax benefits. Still others are good for creating value and a quick sale.

I would like to tell you a secret that most investors ignore: Feel comfortable. Seriously! Ask yourself: "What type of real estate investment makes me comfortable?" It really is different for each person.

In the early 1980s, downtown Fullerton, California, was going through some changes. The city, as well as major developers, started to renovate some of the older properties.

I spoke with city officials as well as developers, real estate brokers, property managers, appraisers, and financial institutions, who all gave me positive feedback.

We bought a twenty-four-unit apartment building that was run down and mismanaged and housed several undesirable tenants. It was, however, directly behind a multimillion dollar project. I rehabbed the property, changed the tenant mix, and sold the building in just over two years at a substantial profit.

In each city or town there are many neighborhoods ready or almost ready for revitalization. Just to name a few examples in Los Angeles: Fairfax and Pico boulevards, Highland and Melrose avenues, and Sunset Boulevard and Vine Street.

Ask yourself: Do I want "pride of ownership" or do I want to rehab or remodel? Do I want to fix and flip, or do I want cash flow and long-term appreciation?

Next, determine what type of asset you want to buy: class A, B, C, D, or E. A good analogy might be to compare A-list properties to A-list celebrities. Do you want everything that comes with inviting an A-list celebrity to your party? If not, it might be better to stick to the C list.

In other words, do you want to invest in low, middle, or upper income areas? What areas can you afford? Where is financing available? What areas provide the greatest return? What type of tenant do you feel comfortable dealing with?

> *Tip from the Coach:*
>
> *When you start, I suggest you consider low- to moderate-income areas.*

When you start, I suggest you consider low- to moderate-income areas. Additionally, when investing in single family homes or apartments, you want properties on a quiet cul-de-sac without high visibility, far away from heavy traffic, railroad tracks, electric high power lines, garbage bins, or storage areas. Yet for retail or commercial properties you want to be in a heavy traffic area and close to public transportation.

In my experience, the quickest way to make your first $1 million is both to fix and flip some properties, and to keep some for cash flow and appreciation. Again, it depends on the location and its potential. Maybe you'd like to build from scratch or convert a property to a different use in order to maximize the return on your investment. Each property type has its advantages and disadvantages. What you choose depends on your personality, your comfort level vis-à-vis your risk reward, and your lifestyle.

As I mentioned before, I began to invest in Mar Vista and the surrounding areas in Southern California: Palms, Venice, Culver City, and Westchester; I then expanded to other areas, from Gardena to Long Beach. Eventually I began to buy in North Hollywood, Van Nuys, Reseda, and Canoga Park. Now I only buy in the A or B Areas: West Los Angeles, Brentwood, Westwood, Santa Monica, Torrance, Glendale, and the Ventura corridor from Calabasas to Toluca Lake, as well as in Arizona, Colorado, Nevada, and Texas.

Now let's take a look at the specific types of properties available for investment.

Residential Properties

One-to-Four Residential Units. Single-family homes (SFHs) and two-to-four residential units are the most popular and the easiest way to invest. They also carry the lowest category of risk in real estate and require the least capital and expertise.

Most investors prefer SFHs or two-to-four residential units when they start. The ideal investment for a beginner is a SFH with two to five bedrooms or a multi-family unit (duplex or fourplex) where the owner/investor can live in one unit and rent out the other units for income.

In fact, up to 80 percent of all money invested in real estate is invested in one-to-four residential units. This draws a lot of competition—and a lot of inexperienced investors.

Fred and Jill came to my seminars a few times and then they went to other seminars many *times, after which they bought several properties in Arizona, Florida, Nevada, and North Carolina. They bought those properties six months after I left those markets. After their purchases, the value of properties in those markets dropped between 40 and 60 percent. Fred and Jill not only lost all of their money—more than $300,000—but they ruined their credit as well.*

In general, when interest rates are low, and the economy is healthy, one-to-four residential units can appreciate reasonably fast. The market will draw a large number of investors and speculators who have no intention of living in those homes. When the market is active, a lot of people make good money. A tight credit market, on the other hand, will affect value and marketability. That's when speculators disappear and the number of transactions is reduced, making prices drop.

Those who buy in a growing market are riding bicycles downhill and often think they're heroes. But when the market slows down or drops, a lot of people lose their shirts. That's why it pays to buy *right*.

One of my associates, Bill, started with one-to-four residential units in the Silver Lake area (near downtown Los Angeles). He used his profits to buy more properties. Now he owns twelve properties and has retired young, living comfortably from the income.

Another client, Ed, started buying one-to-four residential units in low- to moderate-income areas, because they were easier to finance with low down payments and provided for a quick turnaround. He would buy the ugliest property on the street, fix it up, and bring it up to the average property on the block. Now he buys mostly apartment buildings and keeps them for cash flow and appreciation. He found that his time was better spent visiting one building with several units rather than driving from house to house. He also hired an assistant to take care of the day-to-day challenges of property maintenance and dealing with tenants. In less than five years, working part time, he accumulated a small fortune and a nice monthly income from rent.

If you own several properties in a partnership or LLC, one advantage of investing in SFHs is that you can sell each one separately. It's easier to find a buyer for a house or a duplex than for a commercial property. You then have more flexibility to reinvest the money or to use it for other purposes.

The disadvantage of one-to-four residential units is that the cost per unit is higher than a property with ten units or more. Additionally, in most markets rents on these properties are not high enough to justify the price paid or to produce a desirable cash flow.

For example, very few seasoned syndicators bother with SFHs, because the return is low compared to commercial real estate. Small syndicators[1] and beginning investors have no choice, however, because they often are not able to raise the necessary funds. Instead, they assemble several homes or duplexes together and put them into one partnership. However, in a depressed market, because there are so many opportunities, even commercial syndicators who never syndicate single family homes often branch out into that market.

Another disadvantage to SFH investment is that property management is more expensive, as are utilities, gardening, maintenance, and supplies. More importantly, one has to consider not only the return on investment, but also the time the investment requires. You may not be able to afford to hire a resident manager to reduce some of the burden. Plus, most SFH property managers are not experienced and charge more than commercial property managers.

Commercial Properties

Commercial properties typically are income properties consisting of five residential units or more as well as shopping centers, office buildings, industrial buildings, etc. Keep in mind that the valuation of income properties is totally different. So is the financing. Investors and lenders do not only look at sales comparisons, but also at net operating income and internal rates of return (return on investment).

Also keep in mind that management techniques differ substantially for each type of commercial property: retail, office, industrial, apartments, etc. Additionally, long-term leases can limit income potential, but also give more secure income. Long leases with rent escalation clauses are helpful. Tenant improvement and broker commissions will also reduce potential income. However, with commercial properties, leasing agents are more sophisticated, more specialized, and better trained, and management is more professional.

Apartment Buildings. Most investors transition from one-to-four units into small apartment buildings of five-to-fifty units. That's what I did when I started in Lebanon and again in the United States in 1979. I bought one house, then three houses, then several more. Then I quickly transitioned into a fourteen-unit apartment building.

---

[1] Definition: **Syndicator:** *noun* 1. One who syndicates, or pools, group investments to buy real estate. Please see the Glossary for additional real estate terminology.

Some advantages of investing in multi-unit apartment buildings are:

* ❖ You save time (your most valuable asset is your time).
* ❖ More affordable professional management assistance is available.
* ❖ Working with volume saves on labor and supplies.
* ❖ Risk is reduced.
* ❖ There is less competition (due to the fewer opportunities available to purchase commercial properties).

Keep in mind that multi-unit apartment buildings are not as easy as single family homes to buy, finance, and sell: You must sell the building in its entirety and cannot sell a single unit at a time, unless you convert the building into condos. Moreover, apartment buildings are generally more management intensive, yet at the same time are cheaper to maintain. Apartments are a numbers game, however, and the return on your time is generally better.

As with any other real estate investment, location is important when purchasing apartment buildings, but so are timing, trends, price, and management. Never forget that real estate is local. The quality of the immediate neighborhood, accessibility to jobs, schools, and shopping are crucial.

Sam built a small fortune buying and managing apartment buildings. His net income from rent allowed him to retire at age 52 and gave him the opportunity to travel six months a year. Of course, he doesn't manage the buildings himself anymore.

In order to be a *smart investor* in an apartment building, you must learn the answers to some basic questions: What is the rate of absorption (that is, how well is the market absorbing the current inventory of rentals and listings)? How many units are coming onto the market and when? What rent will they be charging? How many units are being converted to condos? What are the job opportunities in the area? What is the average income? Are retirees moving in? If so, into which neighborhoods? Are these retirees potential buyers or potential tenants?

You need to learn how much competition there is for renters. Both new construction and the number of vacant units in the market will affect the performance of your investment. At the same time, however, because there are multiple units in one building, one or two vacancies are not detrimental to your investment. Two vacancies in a twenty-unit building comprise only a 10 percent vacancy rate, while one vacancy in a house means a 100 percent vacancy rate.

Furthermore, if the apartment building produces cash flow, tax segregation might be worthwhile (see Chapter Twelve to learn more about the tax advantages of real estate investment), while for a single family home it may not make sense. Here, the economy of scale affects the return, and purchasing power helps reduce the cost.

Finally, finding a competent property manager is also crucial, since management can make or break your investment. Property managers control tenant retention and relations, the marketing of vacancies, screening of tenants, expense control, and cash flow—all crucial to the success of your project.

Condo Conversions. When the market is hot, even substandard buildings are marketed as potential condo conversions. If the timing is right, you can make money. But if the market is soft, you might lose your shirt. Again, you should do your homework. Research the market, and know what you're doing.

I jointly owned an industrial building in downtown Los Angeles. A major tenant occupying 85 percent of the building moved out. For six months, we were not able to find a tenant. So, in 1984 I became the first investor in the city to convert an industrial building into artists' lofts, which we then sold at substantial profit.

I don't like to build or convert buildings into condos anymore, because the market is saturated. Many developers already have or will soon lose their shirts due to an overabundance of condo conversions.

Historic Buildings. These provide both opportunities and challenges. The positives are that you can buy at a very low cost per unit. Additionally, there are tax investment credits, which are very desirable, because they are direct reductions of tax liabilities. The challenges are that most historic buildings are in tough neighborhoods, which might scare away good tenants. Also, there's cost override: Once you open the walls, you don't know what to expect, and many times there are big surprises inside those walls. Safety codes and other requirements of government regulations might eat up your profit.

Burt bought a historic building in downtown Los Angeles because he was attracted by the potential tax credits. Once he started the renovation, he was faced with several challenges, which caused him to run out of funds. He lost the building to foreclosure.

Mixed-Use Projects. It took me ten years to convince the Los Angeles City Council to allow mixed-use projects. I like them, because they reduce the risk of investment. Now they are even more appealing, because lenders are accepting them as a good form of investment.

Mobile Home Parks. These are similar to apartment units and share many of the same benefits and pitfalls. I have never personally invested in mobile home parks, but I have friends who specialize in this form of investment, because they like the low maintenance, the easy management, and some of the tax benefits. A couple of my friends have converted their mobile home parks into condo mobile home parks.

Office Buildings. Often, a small office building is a safe and rewarding investment. In fact, a small office building in a good, busy location is my favorite type of investment, especially when I am able to attract lawyers, CPAs, insurance agents, real estate brokers, travel agents, chiropractors, dentists, and other professionals to be investors as well as tenants.

Purchasing *large* office buildings, however, is like surfing. If you don't catch the wave at the right time, you will fail. This is the riskiest of all real estate investments, but if you buy at the right time, you will receive a bigger return.

Raw Land. Investment in raw land is usually more speculative than with other types of properties. The return depends on many factors, some of which are beyond the control of the investor. There is no cash

34THE SMART REAL ESTATE INVESTOR'S GUIDE

flow and no tax benefits, except in certain circumstances where there is income from agricultural activities. Land investment in general doesn't generate enough income to cover carrying costs: mortgage, taxes, insurance, etc.

If you choose the right location, within the path of growth, and if you are able to change the zoning, however, the return can be phenomenal. When rezoning, the highest return would come from converting the property to these uses, in this order: 1) office or retail, 2) industrial, 3) residential, and 4) recreational.

Market research and knowing what you are doing are crucial to success with land investment. The local economy, politics, schools, jobs, the direction and limits of growth, local taxes and assessments, zoning, soil, accessibility to utilities, and so on, will all affect your return.

Raw land is a long-term investment; you must be able to carry the mortgage and taxes, otherwise, you may lose your investment. However, I only buy with cash—I never acquire a loan on raw land. Of course, management is very easy with raw land. This is one of the riskiest of real estate investments, but can also be one of the most rewarding.

Self-Storage. These properties fill a need for business and personal use. The trend today is to build smaller homes and condos with limited storage space. People generally tend to keep things they might never need, hence the success of storage facilities. However, self-storage too can be overbuilt, and high vacancies can depress returns. Management of these properties is also relatively easy.

In general, cash flow is dependable with self-storage, and there are some tax benefits. Leases are usually short-term with the potential for high turnover. If you do market research and you know what you're doing, you can make some money.

Shopping Centers. In general, shopping centers provide safe investment opportunities with dependable cash flow and good appreciation. Most leases on shopping centers are NNN, meaning that tenants pay all the expenses, tax, insurance, maintenance, and so on. Many leases have clauses in which the tenants pay, in addition to the fixed rent, a percentage of their gross income.

Special-Use Properties. These are mostly built to suit one type of structure, e.g., a restaurant, gas station, car sales or rental, etc.

Strip Centers and **Small Retail Buildings.** These can be very profitable, but can also be very risky. Location, type and strength of the tenant, and economic conditions all affect the performance of small businesses located in these buildings.

Proper screening of tenants is crucial, not only regarding the financial strength of the tenants, but also the type of business. A mix of businesses will help tenant businesses overall and will help reduce turnover. Management is also important, requiring special attention to details, such as signage, landscaping, and design.

Subsidized Housing. Although this type of property offers an excellent tax write-off, I don't like this form of investment because of the red tape and the restrictions. Unless you are familiar with these types of investments, I don't recommend them.

Warehouses and **Industrial Buildings.** This is a very stable investment, although these types of properties are sensitive to recession. Multi-qualified tenants are a safer investment than a single tenant, or a special-use tenant. If your tenant is a large corporation, remember that even they sometimes go out of business. These properties are far easier to manage, but you have to select the tenants carefully.

However, these properties are good for cash flow and tax benefits. Long-term leases with financially solid companies producing goods that will not become obsolete, and with the potential for regular rent increases, can make these properties very profitable. And if you are in an area where there is potential for conversion to a different use a few years down the line, the return could be phenomenal.

Kurt only buys warehouses. They are easy to manage and are low maintenance. Because he makes sure to buy in good locations, his warehouses are always fully occupied.

Types of Commercial Leases

Gross Leases. With these leases, tenants do not pay any expenses beside their rent. However, sometimes these leases come with variations that include provisions found in the other types of leases listed here.

Some leases are fixed for a certain number of years, with rent increases every three to five years or even ten years. Others have Consumer Price Index (CPI) increases or a certain rate of increase every year. Very few have no rent increase whatsoever.

Long-term Leases. These provide more stability, especially if they have built-in rent increases.

Modified Gross Leases. This is where tenants pay a share of the expenses, but not all. Usually tax and insurance are paid by the owner, and the tenants pay their share of common area expenses, such as utilities, gardening, janitorial, repair, and maintenance.

NNN Leases. Some leases are NNN, in which tenants pay their share of all current and future expenses. In some cases, the owner only pays for the roof and the outside wall maintenance.

Diversification

It's a good idea to diversify your investments only after you have a few properties already under your belt. Once you've gained enough experience, however, diversification of your real estate investments is vital. You might want to diversify and buy different types of properties in different areas, even in different states.

While no market is immune to national economic trends, each market experiences its own unique waves. If you have assets spread through a variety of markets, your overall portfolio is buffered from the gyrations of one particular local market. In other words, while one region may be in a down cycle, another region may be in an up cycle.

The same principle applies to investing in multifamily real estate. By investing in properties outside your market, you geographically diversify your portfolio, allowing you to lower your investment risk and withstand the short-term volatility that is bound to occur.

CHAPTER FOUR

THE ELUSIVE "GOOD BUY": WHERE AND HOW TO FIND IT

*T*he pressing questions most investors have, especially in today's real estate market, are about finding the right properties, in the right locations, for the right prices, and at the right returns. Do you have any of these concerns? Good! Then this book is for you!

Tip from the Coach:

Through the years, I've repeatedly heard a statement that has always proven true:

*You don't make your profit when you **sell** a property; you make the majority of your money when you **buy** a property.*

First, never forget that investing in real estate is one of the best decisions you'll ever make. There are very few purchases you will make in your life that will actually increase in value while you're using them every day.

It's also important to remember that it's actually a GREAT time to buy when the market is soft! As long as you choose a worthwhile property and maintain it well, you'll make good money over the years. Of course, anyone who knows anything about investments will tell you that *smart real estate investors* are in it for the long haul.

Even while the media is saturated with reports of the numbers of properties in foreclosure and how foreclosure rates are increasing at an alarming pace (which will hurt hundreds of thousands of people all over the United States) thousands of great opportunities are being created for able and savvy investors—for you and me.

When both prices and interest rates have fallen, you can lock in a mortgage at a fantastic rate and buy good property below replacement cost. Prices will inevitably rise again, and then you'll be sitting pretty with a great interest rate and extra profit from your amazingly discounted price.

In a soft market, sellers and lenders often have had their properties on the market for longer than they desire, and they may be willing to cut you a deal. That's all the better for you, and the sellers will finally be able to get on with their lives. Everybody wins; especially your pocketbook.

If you're looking to buy a fixer-upper to rent out as an income property, a slow economy will benefit you too. For example, after so many people began losing their homes in the 2007-08 subprime crisis, lenders became leery of handing out properties to people with bad credit, causing a surplus of renters to hit the streets.

But when *is* the right time to buy? I've heard plenty of folks say to wait six months or even a year so prices can drop. Unfortunately, this is not always true. There is no set time frame in which to buy.

Most of us can't predict what interest rates will be in six months or a year. The same holds true for the market; will it be up or will it be down? And if you are waiting for a property's price to hit rock bottom, by the time you recognize that it has, the price is already on its way back up.

So, instead of waiting six months on one property, make several offers on several properties. More often than not, one of those offers will come through at the right price. That way you avoid trying to predict the future.

Keep in mind that you always want to buy below market value. If you're buying at market value, you're not buying right.

So, then, where do you find a good deal? We've all seen the real estate lists. But once a list becomes public, it's too late. It means the sellers are planning to sell at market value. To have a great deal, you must buy at least 20 percent below going market value. However, if you're an expert in a given area, you'll know about the listings before they become public.

Hossein bought several homes in the San Fernando Valley in Southern California. He discovered that the best time to buy was between August and December 2008, because at the time prices were distressed and competition was low.

Another investor, Steve, wanted to buy an office building in foreclosure, but he kept procrastinating, waiting for the market to drop further. When someone else made an offer on the property, he got excited and entered a bidding war. When the other buyer won, Steve was devastated.

The truth is that real estate is cyclical. Yet history teaches us that investing in real estate is always a great decision for the long term. Despite what the media tells you, a slow market is no exception to that rule. There are great buys out there in any market—if you buy *right*.

Learning to Buy Right

As we learned in the last chapter, choosing the type of property in which to invest is crucial. Each type requires a different set of skills and offers different levels of return. Each type of property has its own cycles, temptations, and pitfalls. And each type of property fulfills a different need for you.

Here's a reminder of what you must consider as you're choosing what type of property in which to invest:

❖ Do you know exactly what you want?
❖ Are you choosing an area where you feel comfortable and the type of property that interests you?
❖ Do you understand the risk/reward ratio appropriate for your lifestyle?
❖ Have you become an expert in the area? Do you know the buildings, populations, schools, and politics—all pertinent aspects of an area?

Please note: A person's risk/reward tolerance depends on age, net worth, and tolerance for risk. Real estate is an investment, and the return should be compared to other investments. One should not only consider the cash return and the appreciation, but also the tax benefits and the leverage. I recommend not just taking risks, but taking *calculated* risks.

In general, the younger the person, the more the risk that can be taken. For example: Young people could buy property with a high potential for appreciation and little or no cash flow. They could also buy a property out of state. Older people should buy properties with immediate cash flow as well as potential for appreciation in a market they know well, close to where they live.

Whatever your age, before you make an offer, make sure the property in question is in alignment with your answers to all of the questions below and with all of your criteria.

Of course, those answers will change throughout your career in real estate. What might work for you initially will most certainly change over time as both your know-how and income increase.

> *Tip from the Coach:*
>
> *Sustainable employment growth is the key to property demand.*

Remember: *All real estate is local.* By observing your local market you can identify those opportunities that are within your capacity to act. If you learn to value a property perfectly based on the local market, the condition of the property, your return requirements, and your borrowing power, you'll easily recognize a potentially profitable transaction.

Before you invest in any area, it's essential that you be genuinely convinced of the near- and long-term prospects of the overall real estate market in that location. Is the market stabilizing, going up, or going down? Typically, the best time to invest is when prices and values are still depressed, just before prices and the number of transactions start to rise. Yet it's always a good time to buy when you find a good deal.

It's very important to thoroughly research a market to find out the direction it's taking *before* you invest. Develop a clear picture of the market by reviewing economic and demographic data, job reports, building trends, occupancy data, and past performance.

Always go where the action is. Where people want to live is where you want to invest! Learn the areas where people are moving in and what areas where people are moving away. Look for metro job centers and pay attention to high population growth and commuting distances.

In Southern California, for example, the metro job center stretches from Ventura County to San Diego County. This range has a constantly growing population of five figures, which varies between twelve to twenty million—and its population is expected to double within fifty years! That is exactly the kind of growth that promotes investment opportunity.

> *Tip from the Coach:*
>
> *All real estate is local.*
>
> *There is no general real estate market.*

Next, follow the businesses and you'll find yourself in a good market for investment. Remember, no jobs mean no people and no money. That means no tenants to pay rent and no real estate appreciation.

In general, people move to areas of low-priced real estate where jobs are being created, where there are good schools, good weather, and where people retire. If an area has low job growth but retirees are moving in, the value of real estate will increase. But be aware that government regulations can also affect economic growth and housing prices positively or negatively.

Also keep in mind that great opportunities can be found in markets or submarkets that appear unfavorable. Areas that have suffered economically and from overbuilding in recent years, but have excellent fundamentals for sustained employment growth can be very good places to invest. In each city or town across the nation, there are neighborhoods ready or almost ready for revitalization. They're easy to spot just by driving around or by speaking to city officials, members of the chamber of commerce, property managers, real estate brokers, bankers, CPAs, or lawyers.

All these pieces of information, when put together, are the best indicators for which markets will be hot down the road. And knowing as much as you can about a local market is very important if you plan to be a long-term buy-and-hold investor.

In addition, you must remain persistent and focused. Your odds of success increase when you choose large population centers and *remain* in the market, constantly on the lookout for your type of deal.

Is It Really All About "Location, Location, Location"?

What does the well-worn phrase "location, location, location" actually mean? How important is it? In my experience, it's only part of success in real estate investment. Location, trends, and timing are all very important. Location is a key that opens the door to successful investment if the economic picture and timing are also right.

Gene bought an office building in a great location in downtown Austin, Texas. However, the timing wasn't good, because he purchased just before the recession began. Gene ended up losing his shirt.

Without a doubt, location *is* important. It's the one aspect of a property you cannot change. You can make updates to a building and replace some or all of the tenants, but you can't change the neighborhood. Keep in mind that it's also very difficult and expensive to change the structure of a building.

Once you buy, you're stuck with the surrounding area, for better or for worse. In many ways you are at the whim of the location you've chosen—so it's essential that you choose carefully!

Jora purchased an apartment building in Atlanta, Georgia, without ever visiting the site and found himself saddled with some tenants who were bad and dangerous. The property was in poor condition and in an undesirable area of town—a location where Jora should never have purchased a property. By the time he closed escrow, the building was half empty. The cost of rehabbing was much more than anticipated, and it was not easy to find tenants. Jora ended up losing a lot of money and lost the property to foreclosure.

In the long run, properties in better locations appreciate much faster than in mediocre locations. The drawback, of course, is the significantly larger initial investment necessary to secure a property in an obviously desirable neighborhood. Your rate of return will be lower, but so is the risk.

In choosing a good location, you have two options: selecting what is currently a prime location or choosing property in an area that has *the potential* to become excellent, but is not there yet. Selecting a prime location is beneficial, because those property values increase most rapidly when the market goes up and decrease last and least when property prices drop.

Barry went to a seminar, where an articulate, experienced salesman (not a real estate expert) pressured him into buying that night. He purchased a house still under construction in Fort Worth, Texas. He took possession, and a year later the house was still vacant. The value of the property today is a third of what it was when he bought it.

Remember that apartment building I bought in Fullerton? (See Chapter Three.) It was run down, mismanaged, and rented to undesirable tenants. But it was in a great location, directly behind a multi-million-dollar new development project in an up-and-coming area, so it made investment sense.

> *Tip from the Coach:*
>
> ***Success in real estate comes through right* locations, trends, *and* timing.**

Of course, the best cities in which to invest typically have barriers that effectively curb expansion. For example, on the coasts there is always at least one barrier to the expansion of a city, which allows the most drastic appreciation of the properties located there. In Los Angeles, I always choose to invest on properties that lie west of Interstate 405, because the ocean to the west curtails growth and makes it a very desirable area. If a desirable area can't expand, then property values naturally rise.

On the other hand, avoid buying property in the middle of nowhere. You'll encounter many advertisements purporting to be incredible deals—in the papers, on the radio or TV, on the Internet, and even at special functions at luxury hotels.

Bill bought a piece of land in West Texas, sight unseen. Without exaggeration, we drove six hours from Dallas and searched for another hour without seeing anything except plains and tumbleweeds. When we finally found someone to ask for help, the gentleman told us quite a few people, like us, were looking for similar property—and never found it.

You might laugh at the stories of people falling for these sales

gimmicks, but they're absolutely true! Those in-the-boondocks properties are advertised all the time, especially on TV in the middle of the
night, so be careful!

Location is also issue of practicality. If you're planning to manage a
property yourself and be active in the day-to-day operations, it's
essential you buy something close to where you live and work. Don't
buy properties more than an hour away from your home or business if
you want to do the work yourself—no matter how tempted you might
be.

Obviously, if you plan to hire a professional property management
company or are working with a long-distance partner, proximity is not
a major consideration. In those cases, financial viability becomes your
sole concern.

*Nicky's inexperience led him to buy two homes in North Carolina,
where an entire subdivision of 360 homes was sold to investors. He
bought them at the wrong time. They were very difficult to rent, and
in a year prices had dropped by 60 percent. Nicky had to give back
the houses to the lender, lost his money, and ruined his credit.*

The drawbacks to a long-distance approach stem from your
potential unfamiliarity with a given area. Therefore, research becomes
imperative—do your homework! Analyze carefully which state, towns,
and neighborhoods display idyllic market trends.

In addition, you must make *absolutely sure* someone trustworthy is
on-site and available to contribute directly to daily operations—
someone who's in your corner. At the very least, you'll need a property
management company with impeccable credentials and a reliable
reputation.

To invest in today's market, you either need to know exactly what
you're doing or work with experienced people, or both. And make sure
you work only with people you can depend on and trust!

Not long ago, many investors bought properties in Arizona, Florida,
Nevada, Texas, or the Carolinas—at the wrong time. People who
bought in certain areas of California, such as Riverside, San Bernar-

dino, Palmdale, Lancaster, and the Central Valley (Bakersfield to Sacramento) also lost money. What do all the above areas have in common? They entered a period of a very high rate of foreclosure. What happens to home prices when an area has a lot of foreclosures? They tumble, of course. What about rents? They drop as well.

In 1979, I saw a newspaper ad for a thirty-two unit apartment building on Sepulveda Boulevard in West Los Angeles.

I had been scouting the area for several months. Based on my knowledge of area property values, I realized that the building was priced well below market value. I called the owner immediately and set up a meeting within the hour at his house in Malibu.

I brought a $10,000 check with me made out to an escrow company of the seller's choice, and, of course, a written offer. The owner reduced the price, because he wanted a quick sale and close. He had built the property twenty-two years before, had managed it himself, and had made good money. It was a good time to move on, considering his health and age.

I offered him full asking price and a quick close with very simple, clear terms and conditions. No games, tricks, or creative contingencies. He accepted the offer and signed the contract.

The following day, he received several offers, some of them much higher than mine. Three of those buyers tried to purchase the property from me for $200,000-$300,000 more than I had paid.

Once you've thoroughly done your homework and you've chosen a market, you'll want to quickly become an expert in that market. Learn all you can about the economy, the real estate industry, and what's going on in the neighborhood of your choice.

However, you do *not* want to wait until you become expert to start investing. Why? Because procrastination is the biggest enemy of success. A supposedly good excuse will not lead to success, i.e., "I don't have the money." "I don't have the time." "I don't have the experience." "I don't know where to start."

Noel was a nice guy from a wealthy family who never focused on much of anything. One day he got the idea that he wanted to be a real estate developer like me. He went about it like many other things in his life: without doing his homework. He bought a piece of prime real estate on Main Street in Santa Monica, California. His idea was to build a three-story building with a restaurant and offices. He found someone who worked with an architect to draw up plans based on his ideas. This person was not an actual architect, because Noel was too cheap to pay an experienced professional! As the building project progressed, Noel ran out of money, and his banker refused to extend further credit. The bank asked my advice. I soon discovered that the planning was extremely poor, and the building was completely unsuitable for any kind of operations. It should never have been built in the first place. Noel lost the building to the bank.

It's not only the great ideas that help *smart investors* make their first million, but great ideas with *actions*. So whenever you have a good idea, or you hear about a great idea that you like, jot it down and take immediate action. The longer you wait, the more you'll miss out on your opportunities.

Remember: There are opportunities in *every* market. When the market is hot, there's more competition, meaning that opportunities come fewer and far between, but there will always be people who must sell for one reason or another. It's up to you to find them. You'll have much better luck finding good deals if you identify one or more desirable locations and get to know the value of the diverse properties there. If you're working with real estate brokers, you can ask them which listings must close within thirty days.

However, *never* develop properties without properly doing your homework or seeking advice from an experienced consultant.

Beginning Your Search for Viable Properties

Through the years I have dealt with more than two thousand buyers and sellers. Almost always, sellers want to sell properties at more than market value, and buyers want to buy properties at less than market value. That means if you want to get a good deal, you must do the following:

1. Know the market so you'll recognize a bargain when you see it.
2. Screen properties quickly to weed out unprofitable deals. This should be done not only by crunching numbers, but also through experience, good judgment, and a thorough knowledge of the market.
3. Analyze a prospective property by focusing on a few important issues. If you take the time to analyze a property completely, the opportunity will be long gone.
4. Be able and willing to quickly make a decision to purchase.
5. Take action faster than everyone else. If the numbers make sense, make your offer, and make sure you keep it simple. Sign the contract and pay the deposit. (However, be ready to make fast course change if you must. Don't let somebody swindle you into buying a lemon property.)

> *When a reporter asked the famous hockey player, Wayne Gretzky, "How come you always go where the puck is?"—he responded, "No, no! I don't do that at all. I don't go where the puck is; I go where the puck is going to be!"*

As Stephen Covey says, "Start with the end in mind." Even before you begin your search for investment properties, think of your exit strategy and to whom you will sell.

Always assess a property's sales potential before buying it, even if you plan to hold it for years. Ask yourself, "If I sell this building tomorrow or as soon as I create value, will I make a profit?" If the answer is no, walk away; don't even consider it.

Of course, you don't have to reinvent the wheel to be ahead of the game. Rather, you can go where successful investors and related professionals go. But be sure to follow them at the beginning, when they start to develop or invest, not when they're selling and starting to leave.

Finding the Ideal Seller

Finding that first (or latest) great deal, i.e., locating a property on which to make an offer, isn't as hard as you might think. First, think about people who must sell for one reason or another. These include people in foreclosure, the recently divorced, those who must move out of state, those who have had a death in the family, people who must move for health reasons, those who have lost their jobs, someone who received the property as an inheritance and doesn't want to keep it, or those who are just fed up with owning a property. These property owners will often sell at 15 to 20 percent below market value. For one reason or another, they want to, or must, sell quickly.

Some indications of a motivated seller are:

- ❖ High vacancy rates
- ❖ Tax problems
- ❖ Divorce or other family problems
- ❖ Negative cash flow (not enough reserves)
- ❖ Run-down or distressed property
- ❖ Distressed market, changes in the economy, loss of jobs
- ❖ Long-distance owner
- ❖ A pending move
- ❖ Signs of mismanagement
- ❖ Obvious tenant problems
- ❖ Dissolution of a partnership
- ❖ Lack of skill and/or desire to manage
- ❖ Health problems
- ❖ Advanced age or death
- ❖ Over-priced property (initially paid too much)
- ❖ Seller asking for unrealistically high down payment
- ❖ Old listing
- ❖ Past due assessments

Remember: Good buys come from doing your homework. You can buy lists, look at your county recorder's office, scour the local newspapers, and (especially) use the Internet. In doing so, you can come across some very motivated sellers.

Strategies for Finding Good Buys

Below is a list of practical ways to get information about properties for sale:

Advertising. Advertise that you buy real estate. Consider using the following resources:

- The Internet
- Billboards
- Bumper stickers
- Flyers
- Phone books
- Radio
- Street benches
- TV

You can post flyers at colleges, coin-operated laundries, shopping centers, bowling alleys, public bulletin boards, churches, local businesses, and on street poles (including poles at freeway exits).

Auctions. Your best chance to limit competition and get the property at a rock-bottom price is to attend auctions when the weather is bad or those at which the property absolutely must be sold. If there is no reserve on what can be accepted (no lowest price limit), you may win big.

Banks and Financial Institutions. Let local lenders, banks, and other financial institutions know you're buying foreclosures and ask about their OREO properties (Other Real Estate Owned). If you pre-qualify with them beforehand, they may call you sooner. Also ask them for leads on properties in distress, before or during the foreclosure process.

When you do negotiate with the officer of a bank regarding a property, don't nickel-and-dime them. Make them look good, and you'll often be generously rewarded. I've obtained some great bargains from several banks and savings and loans institutions because I made the officers look good.

I bought a twenty-seven unit apartment building from Columbia Savings and Loan. To save face with his employer, the officer underwriting the loan needed a certain price for the property. Although my offer was 30 percent below market, I accepted his counteroffer at 10 percent under market—provided he gave me a loan at below market financing with only a 20 percent down payment.

I saved more money than if I had insisted on my original offer. In addition, the officer offered me first right of refusal on several other properties from which I made over half a million dollars.

Bird Dogs. These are people, or in some cases companies, who locate properties for investors. The best bird dogs have a ton of contacts within their respective markets. They also know a good property when they see one. Bird dogs seek out relationships with brokers, agents, bankers, and anyone else that may have knowledge of a good deal on real property.

How do bird dogs get paid? Once an investor buys the property, the bird dog is paid a finder's fee, which is typically a percentage of the transaction or a flat fee. Some bird dogs command rates as high as 10 percent. I've heard of higher fees, but most finder's fees run in the 3 to 6 percent range.

Cash Incentives. Everyone you know should know you'll give them $500 if a referral leads to you buying a property. Print up cards that say "I pay $500 to $5,000 to you at closing if I buy a house you told me about. Do you know anyone who is selling property? Please call [your name] at [your phone number]."

Possible soldiers in your cash incentives army can include:

❖ Acquaintances
❖ CPAs
❖ Friends and relatives
❖ Gardeners

- ❖ Landlords
- ❖ Landscapers
- ❖ Lawyers
- ❖ Mail carriers
- ❖ Moving companies
- ❖ Neighbors
- ❖ Other investors
- ❖ Paperboys
- ❖ Pest control company personnel
- ❖ Property managers
- ❖ Relocation services
- ❖ Service technicians
- ❖ Tenants
- ❖ Your organizations

Please note: Water, gas, and electric company personnel can be very good when it comes to finding vacant or distressed properties.

Give each of your soldiers stacks of your business cards and then watch for exponential growth in your referrals.

Developers in Distress. Developers who are eager to move on to the next project are often willing to sell at a discount. Sometimes you can get a bargain by buying properties before or during construction. Another good source for finding developers is through government agencies.

Discounted Notes. I have purchased several notes at a discount from lenders. I made money on the notes, and whenever I had to foreclose, I made even more money. However, be careful when you buy a note from the lender. You are not buying the *property*, you're only buying the lender's position, and there could be other liens or debt on the property that cut into your profit.

In 1998, I bought thirty-two units under construction in Toluca Lake, California. The developer had run out of money when the building was just three-quarters complete. Although the capital invested was $800,000, he accepted just $50,000 in order to save his credit.

Foreclosures and Notices of Default. Research notices of defaults and foreclosures and then contact the owners or lenders. You can buy specialized lists that will show the foreclosure listings of banks and other financial institutions as well as private lenders and government agencies.

Let local lenders know that you're buying foreclosures. If you pre-qualify with them beforehand, they may call you sooner. Ask for leads on properties in distress, before or after the lenders foreclose on the properties. Foreclosures are discussed in more detail in Chapter Eight.

Internet. Using the World Wide Web is one of the hottest ways to find distressed properties. It's amazing how much you can find out about a given property just by going online.

Network. Join various groups and associations. There are organizations for apartment builders, apartment owners, apartment managers, real estate investment clubs, etc. Get to know the people involved. In the process, you'll meet people with properties they want to sell or who are interested in buying the properties you want to sell.

Attend seminars about real estate, not only to learn about investing, but also to circulate among real estate-minded people and find mentors. I met Joe at the apartment association meeting, for example. We became friends, and he eventually bought three apartment buildings from me.

Once you've obtained the names and contact information of several key people, start your own club meetings.

Don't forget to talk to your friends, family, business associates, and just people you meet. Let them know what you're looking for.

Don't count out senior citizens! They tend to know what's going on in their neighborhood and are often valuable informants. Not only do they know the neighborhood gossip, they often need people to talk to. Listen to them!

Newspapers. To get a jump on your competition, be one of the first to receive copies of a newspaper right off the press. You can also build a relationship with someone who works at the press who can give you the information before the editions are printed.

Don't forget to search small, independent (often free) publications as well as the area's major publications.

Look in the "Real Estate" or "Home" sections for foreclosure auctions, tax sales, and HUD and VA properties.

Look in the "Legal" section and contact heirs and their attorneys.

Look in the "Garage Sales" or "Estate Sales" sections. Up to 20 percent of those advertising garage and estate sales are planning to move soon. Go to a garage sale and ask about the homeowner's house or neighbor's homes.

Look in the "Classifieds" section for homes for sale by owners.

Properties in Probate. Looking for properties in probate is an excellent way to find bargains. Some of the nation's wealthiest families get entangled in probate procedures. No matter how much money people may have, when something is bequeathed to them they may be anxious to get their hands on the funds. They may gladly sell the real estate at a significant discounted price just to get the cash.

Real Estate Agents. Real estate agents can give you excellent referrals, but remember: they'll always try to sell you something! Therefore, be very specific about what you want, and tell them to call only if they have properties that meet your investment criteria.

Ask agents to give you pocket listings, long listings, and expired listings.

Pocket Listings. These refer to the time lapse between when the agent first acquires a listing and when the property is actually marketed to the public. Having the listing before anybody else does gives you an edge on the competition.

Tom worked for a large real estate firm in Dallas. He helped me buy two buildings there before they were put on the market. The seller was out of state and wanted a quick close. Tom knew we could close fast. We closed the deal in less than thirty days, although Tom's firm generally takes thirty days just to prepare the marketing package.

Long Listings. Ask for listings that have been on the market for sixty days or longer, or properties that are recently back on the market. A property that has been difficult to sell may be a bargain in disguise.

Expired Listings. Since the real estate agent couldn't sell the property, suggest a 2 percent commission if they'll assist with the closing paperwork after you make a deal with the seller on your own.

As your investment business grows, you can offer agents bigger commissions to help you find great properties.

The Streets. Hit those streets! You can drive or walk by the area where you've chosen to invest. Watch for abandoned or damaged properties. Look for signs of distress or neglect, such as tall or dry grass, weeds, chipped paint, broken fences, and boarded-up or broken windows. Also look for properties that have been victims of fire, earthquake, or flood. They could turn out to be a great bargain.

Talk to the neighbors of such properties; they usually know what's going on with a nearby home, and they also have an interest in seeing it restored.

Walk up to a property and look in the windows to confirm it is vacant, but don't endanger yourself by getting bitten by the family dog or shot at by a suspicious owner or tenant. (And remember, you're not allowed to look in the mailbox to see who's receiving mail.) Always remember to leave your card at the door if no one is home. If you discover that the owners are out of state, you can call or write to them by searching for contact information in property records.

Tax Sales. A friend of mine, Simon, made millions by building on properties he acquired in tax sales. In California, tax sales don't happen often enough, but that's not true in most other states, often meaning that tax sales a way to find a good bargain.

Unfavorable Markets. This fact bears repeating: Excellent opportunities can be found in a market that appears unfavorable. Areas that have suffered economically and from overbuilding but have excellent fundamentals for sustained employment growth (the key to real estate appreciation) can prove to be ripe for profitable investment.

In May 2009, the Las Vegas real estate market was still very depressed. I helped Elie buy five homes at 35 percent of the value they had been three years before. He put 20 percent down and sold the houses within five months at 20 percent above the price he had paid for them, thus doubling his money.

Close That Deal!

It's not until you close the deal that you start making money. First, make sure that you fully understand the closing process. Then, when you're sure you've finally found a property that promises to be a great investment, do everything within your power to bring the deal to a quick and complete close.

Once your deal closes, you'll either get paid a nice chunk of money, or you'll own a new property. But either way, you have to close to get there.

CHAPTER FIVE

ANALYZE THE MARKET, *THEN* THE INVESTMENT

*H*ow many of you have children? If so, you know that one of the major things we try to accomplish as parents is for our children to learn from our mistakes so they can avoid them in their own lives. I have been in the real estate investment business for more than forty years and, yes, I have made my share of mistakes. My hope is that the information in this book will be a way for you to learn from my mistakes and glean from my experiences, so you too can become a *smart real estate investor.*

There is no better place to expand on that idea than when talking about analyzing the market and the investment, because, of course, what properties you choose to buy and where are crucial to your ultimate success or failure as a real estate investor.

First, Review Your Goals

Once you have found that first (or tenth or fiftieth) good buy, that one you've been searching for, there is yet another step to take before you make a specific offer (and counter-offers, as they come): You must also thoroughly analyze both the local market and the investment.

But before you do that, pause for a moment and once again ask yourself what your goals are, what you want to achieve, and how soon you want to achieve them. Doing so will help you stay focused and help to ensure that you are meeting your set objectives.

Second, Analyze the Market

After you've selected an area and the type and class of property in which you really want to invest, you must find the answers to the following questions:

- Is the *area* class A, B, or C?
- Is the *property* class A, B, or C?
- Are you purchasing a value-added property, or are you purchasing for cash flow?
- How many properties are for sale in the area?
- What is the average length a property stays on the market in the area before it is sold?
- What is the average asking price for properties in the area?
- What are the sales comps (sales prices for comparable properties)?
- What properties have been sold at asking price, for more than asking price, or for less than asking price?
- For how much more or less were they sold?
- What are the area's occupancy rates? What is the trend—higher or lower occupancies?
- Are rents increasing or decreasing? Why?
- How much competition is there for tenants in the area?
- What types of tenants are living in the building? What types of tenants will you be able to attract?

And don't forget to check with the planning department to find out the number of buildings under construction and how many are still on the drawing board in the area. Many fortunes in real estate have been lost because of overbuilt markets.

In other words, you have to be an expert in your area. I've said it before, and I'll say it again: Do your homework! If you're an expert in your area then you'll know what the market is like, you'll know how properties are priced and at what price they're sold, and you'll have a better idea of where to look and what to offer.

Third, Analyze the Investment

Even if you have found a good property it doesn't mean you've found a good deal. Yes, there are good deals (even steals) out there, but you must be careful. Remember, buying cheap can end up being very expensive!

So, let's start with the basics. Before you waste much time considering a property, you should evaluate its physical condition and setting. As you're selecting an area and the type and class of property, watch for red flags:

- ❖ Will there be any concessions offered during the sale? What will those concessions be?
- ❖ Is the building under rent control?
- ❖ Are there any special taxes or assessments that might affect the return?
- ❖ Are there any special taxes or assessments that might affect the sale of the property?
- ❖ Is there a utilities assessment?
- ❖ Is the building individually metered or master metered? (Who pays the utilities, the tenant or the owner?)

A friend of mine bought a small house in the Brentwood neighborhood of Los Angeles for a great price. It was only 1,250 square feet, but he had aspirations of expanding it or tearing it down and building a new 4,000 square-foot home. On the surface it was perfect, so he purchased the property for a hefty sum. But he didn't put in his due diligence.

The house turned out to have been built by a famous architect. It was a protected property. That meant not only could my friend not do a tear down, he couldn't expand or make major changes. He couldn't even move the house at his own expense. He was stuck with it as it was.

He came to me for help, but it was already too late. There was nothing we could do. If he had done his homework, if he had been an expert in that particular area, he could have avoided the problem altogether.

Different states have different real estate rules, but so do different communities, even individual lots. You have to know the jurisdiction and the zoning. You have to know the environmental restrictions and any historical protections.

An all-too-often overlooked aspect of market analysis is the land survey. About 99 percent of novice investors fail to get land properly surveyed. You can't rely solely on the title report, which means you must make the land survey one of the contingencies in your offer. (For example, easements aren't always disclosed in title reports.)

A few years ago a group of investors and I were planning to buy land outside of San Antonio Texas. The land next to the parcel was being built up with fourplexes. Our plan was to do the same thing on our land, and we were told we could do so. The title report showed no problems.

But my experience told me to request a survey. That survey showed that we wouldn't be able to build sixty-four fourplexes (as was our plan and as we had been told by the seller and his broker) but only fourteen! With that knowledge, we knew it was a bad deal, and we pulled out only ten days before closing. We lost some money, but saved ourselves a small fortune.

When it comes to analyzing the market and the investment, there is nothing more important to your success than putting in your due diligence. I've said so many times, but I cannot stress the point enough.

Karim's "*Smart* Investment" Formula

In addition to doing my homework and completing a financial analysis of the property and the local market, I buy differently from most people—using the asking price only as a guide. I look at property location, neighborhood, quality of construction, floor plans, and amenities. Then I look at how much improvement the property needs and estimate the cost of improvements and the time it will take to complete them.

Then I ask myself the following questions: When do I expect to sell the property? What will the selling price be? How much money will the property generate during the holding period? How much will the property cost me during the holding period? How much profit do I want to make?

I add that all together and add 20 percent of my expected profit (in case I made a mistake), then I discount the figure to determine how much I should pay the seller. And I always leave room for negotiation.

For example, if the price I'm willing to pay is $1,400,000 I make my first offer at $1,290,000 or $1,335,000. It all depends on the information I have gathered about the seller and the property. And, yes, sometimes I offer 30 to 40 percent less. Rarely do I offer full price. It all depends on the asking price vis-à-vis the value.

The formula helps me determine if what I plan to offer for a property makes investment sense.

Inspect and Analyze the Records

As you use the formula I've outlined above and you're crunching numbers to determine the viability of a property, do your homework— your due diligence. Do a thorough inspection of the property, the books, and records. Find out what needs to be done, how much the repairs will cost, how long will it take to sell, the current cost, how much you can sell the property for, and how much you want to make in profit.

Also compare property values and rents. The best way to measure a property's market value is to compare it to the sales prices of nearby properties. Check the vacancies and the absorption and rental rates of similar properties in the neighborhood. Compare sales per square foot and per door, the gross multiplier, the CAP rate, and the internal rates of return.

Larry made an offer on an apartment building in the South Bay region of Southern California. Upon completing the due diligence, he discovered that the rents were 15 percent above market due to special concessions given to the tenants. For new tenants, he would have had to lower the rents. Of course, Larry walked away from the deal.

Before you invest, be sure to address the following: equity pay down, tax benefits, cash flow, capital appreciation, and pride of ownership. Be careful to avoid negative cash flow; property that eats your cash every day may lead to financial problems, frustration, and stress. Cash flow problems may also make you sell your investment before the benefits of ownership are ever realized.

It should go without saying that when you drop your hard-earned money into real estate, always use sound business judgment. Remember that buying right means buying at 70 to 80 percent of current market value or lower. How do you find out what the market value is? Check the tax rolls for the property you are interested in; many of them are available online. If you are unable to find them online, check with your realtor.

Additionally, have your realtor run a Comparative Market Analysis (CMA) as this is the best indicator of market value. It will reveal what similar properties in the area have sold for. Have your realtor run the analysis for the last six months, as recent sales are better indicators of current market value for your investment analysis.

Richard bought an apartment building in North Carolina. He had never visited the building nor had he ever visited North Carolina. The cost of rehabbing and repairing the building was seven times more than he had been told by his real estate broker and property manager. Richard could not afford the cost of repairs and was not able to convince an investor to help. He ended up losing the building to the bank and ruined his credit.

Remember that the broker's proforma is a projection of the property's operation under the most *ideal* of circumstances with location, condition, and occupancy, which is reflected by the asking price. These are not the real numbers or the effective income and expenses and are not necessarily reflective of what's actually happening at the property.

Your first challenge, then, is to buy the property at a price that reflects its *current* condition. Your job during the due diligence is to figure out what is really going on with the property so you can buy it for what it is actually worth—"As Is"—not what it will be worth after you've spent your time and money on it.

I've been in the real estate investment business full time, full service since 1963, before many of those reading this book were born. Keep in mind that I'm a broker, and yet over the years I've seen very few real numbers from sellers of cash flow properties. Invariably, the owners or their agents are quite optimistic; they seem to always add to the income from a property and somehow miss some of the expenses. So be careful when you're analyzing a property.

When buying a multi-family or commercial property, you should look at all of the leases, especially for the last twelve months. And make sure they are *real* leases, not bogus ones. Also look at the applications and what the previous owners/managers did to screen tenants.

> ### Tip from the Coach:
>
> ### *When you smell something wrong—when your gut feeling tells you something isn't right— walk away!*

For example, some investors and I inspected a property in San Antonio that we were told was 94 percent occupied. When we checked the numbers, however, the collection rate was 58 percent. Running into a circumstance like that means that you can't be afraid to walk away when you don't feel comfortable. When you smell something wrong, when your gut feeling tells you something isn't right—walk away.

Another important document to obtain is the owner's business tax return, including Schedule E, which lists the property's income and expenses. I don't accept less than two years of tax returns. In fact, several times I have refused to purchase a property because the seller refused to show me the Schedule E.

I found out through experience that very few sellers will give the IRS more money than they have to—so the real income should be listed on the Schedule E. One seller once told me, "Last year we had a bad year; this year will be better." But I want to buy the property for how it's valued today, not what it's going to be. I buy properties to *create* value; I don't want to pay for value that's not there.

In addition to two years of tax returns, ask the broker or the seller to provide the Statement of Income and Expenses and Statement of Profit and Loss for year-to-date and the previous year, detailed by each month and signed by the seller or his CPA. That way you can track any unusual expenses and ask questions.

Next, ask for the current rent roll, which will show you exactly how many units are occupied and exactly what each tenant pays in rent. It will also tell you unpaid rents and concession losses. Also ask for a list of capital improvements and any major repairs made during the last two years. You should also obtain a list of capital improvements needed currently. Find out how many loans there are on the property and the current balance of each. With that information, you can ascertain the Net Operating Income (NOI), which you can then track month by month for trends.

I bought a sixty-unit apartment building in Torrance, California. The rent roll showed only three vacancies. When I inspected the building and discovered that there were actually eleven vacant units, I was able to renegotiate the purchase price.

Documentation to ask for from the sellers includes:

- ❖ Leases for the past twelve months
- ❖ Tenant applications and screening procedures
- ❖ Tax returns, specifically Schedule E, for the past two years
- ❖ Income and Expense Statement, year-to-date and previous year detailed by month
- ❖ Profit and Loss Statement, year-to-date and previous year, detailed by month
- ❖ Current Rent Roll, showing unoccupied units, unpaid rents, and concession losses

❖ List of Capital Improvements for the past two years
❖ Documentation of any loans against the property

Finally, never rely on the information the sellers give you. Verify everything, even if you know and trust the sellers. In many instances a seller will claim the rents are higher and the expenses are lower, and a few of them do so unintentionally. Within the documentation, look carefully at the declared income. From that information, you can determine what constitutes a good investment for you and how much you are willing to offer.

Most buyers go by the asking price. But let's say the asking price for a property is $2 million, and the seller accepts $1.8 million. Some investors think they've got a good buy. Wait a minute! The property might only be worth $1.4 million. So make your offers based on your analysis of the property and not on the broker's proforma or the asking price. You'll only know if you've truly got a good deal if you've done your homework.

The market has changed a lot recently, and it's still changing. But that makes investing in real estate all the more enticing—if you know what you are doing.

Avoiding Pitfalls

Finally, when making your investment decision be sure to watch out for obvious pitfalls, such as the following:

Beware the Typical Red Flags. When making an investment purchase decision, properties to avoid under almost any circumstance are ones with foundation or structural problems, negative drains (water running back into the property), or those that are uninsurable. Very few buyers are going to give you an extra $15,000 to $20,000 above your asking price because you have replaced things that they cannot see.

Beware Illegal Conversions. Another pitfall to avoid is the illegal conversion. These days you see a lot of commercial conversions, such as apartment buildings or hotels; I have even seen a garage space converted to office space. But you must be careful about conversions. In fact, you can easily run into a situation when you're looking at an investment property in which you discover that one or more of the units are not legal.

It pays to be careful. Check the history of the property. If there have been conversions, whether to an apartment building or single family home or commercial property, if those conversions have not been permitted, then buyer beware. And as an investor who buys a property and completes upgrades or additions without getting permits and then sells the property, you can be liable, even years later. That's why before I buy I consult a lawyer to check the legalities.

A friend of mine converted a garage into a residential rental, creating a room with a kitchen and other living facilities. The tenant paid the first and last month's rent—and that's all he paid. Four months later, my friend tried to sue him for the rent. But he couldn't collect, because the unit was illegal. Not only that, the tenant was over seventy years old. Because of the laws in Los Angeles, my friend had to pay the tenant more than $8,000 in order to evict him.

Something similar happened to me in West Los Angeles. We purchased a building that had been converted from a two bedroom to a single (bachelor) and a one bedroom. Because the conversion had been done without permits, the city forced us to convert the unit back. Not only did we lose the rent, we also had to pay a relocation fee of $3,500 to each of the four tenants.

PART III:
PRACTICAL ASPECTS
OF REAL ESTATE
INVESTING

CHAPTER SIX

CREATE VALUE IN YOUR INVESTMENT PROPERTIES—IN *ANY* ECONOMY

*W*hy do people go into business? Profit is the strongest motivator for most business people. Real estate investment is a business; therefore you should treat and respect it as a business that must make a profit. Fortunately, the profit potential of a value-added property investment is considerable.

> ### *Tip from the Coach:*
>
> *If real estate investment is so easy, why doesn't everyone do it? And why isn't everyone who has tried it successful? It's because of a lack of commitment, persistence, knowledge, and real desire.*

Still, in the forty-odd years that I have been in real estate, I have continually had people come to me and lament that nothing they have tried works. When people are that negative, impatient, and lacking in patience, it's no wonder that nothing works out for them.

Friends, you can find a million excuses for why you cannot be successful. If you fail, the reason is most likely your attitude and lack of commitment.

I truly believe that anyone with common sense, a real desire, and a good system to follow can be successful. With value-added investments in particular, you must remain positive, because you are putting so much of your own effort into a project.

So, how *do* you create value in real estate? By restoring commercial, retail, industrial, or residential properties that have been allowed to deteriorate through lack of adequate maintenance, through mismanagement, or via abandonment.

The idea is to add value to an existing structure and increase the value beyond the cost of the work.

Rehabbing mismanaged and deteriorating structures is fast becoming the *dominant* form of real estate investing. Some other terms for this process are "buying a fixer-upper" or "fixing and flipping," although you don't have to sell a property immediately in order to benefit from added value.

More and more people are willing to rehab, remodel, or even convert properties to a different use in order to maximize the value of those properties.

Why I Specialize in Value-Added Properties

It's because of the excellent profit potential that I *specialize* in value-added properties—both residential and commercial—meaning that I don't have to depend solely upon appreciation to make a profit. In other words, my company, Dynamics Capital Group, buys wholesale properties to fix up, rent, or resell at a retail price.

My company fills a niche in the marketplace that is absolutely essential. Bank foreclosures, families broken apart by divorce, owners in trouble who need to raise capital quickly: All of them contact us because we are ready buyers. So do brokers, attorneys, and lenders. They are constantly offering us troubled properties or those the sellers absolutely need to sell.

For example, I recently have worked on adding value to small office buildings between 7,000 and 30,000 square feet, mixed use or just offices.

Professionals love to have their offices in a busy area with heavy traffic. Most of my investors have been CPAs, doctors, insurance and real estate brokers, and lawyers. Most of them became tenants as well.

Because many professionals are looking to reduce their rent for office space, I can work with prospective tenants to buy a building together. When your tenants are also your investors, you've got a great investment. The advantages are that your building is 100 percent occupied on day one, and you'll rarely have vacancies.

In fact, there are many ways of earning from such an investment. In one deal on a property between Sepulveda and Santa Monica boulevards in Los Angeles, five of us bought an office building. I'm a broker, so I received a broker commission. I'm managing the property, so I get a management fee. And if I sell the property later, I can make up to 20 percent in profit.

I got several people together plus myself to buy a building near Century City in Los Angeles. The building was run down and only 50 percent occupied. The owner had passed away, and his heirs were fighting, so we picked up the property from the court.

One of the investors was a doctor who was paying $4.25 per square foot for office space; his landlords were about to raise his rent to $4.75 per square foot. I asked him if he could find another friend to invest. He found two friends.

Now, as tenant/owners they're paying each other $3.25 per square foot, $1.75 less than where they were before. Plus, we added value to the property. Everyone is happy.

During my forty-plus years in business, I have bought and rehabbed more than a thousand properties. They have ranged from single-family homes, apartments, mixed-use projects, retail and industrial buildings, to straightforward office buildings. It takes time to do it right, however. On average, for every fifty properties I examine, I end up buying one.

To illustrate how it works, suppose you purchase an undervalued property for $200,000. You put in $25,000 to make repairs, update the property, add features, and improve the landscaping, plus you spend $20,000 in carrying costs. You beautify the property inside and out, and after you finish, sell the property for $345,000.

Subtract the $25,000 you put into fixing up the property, the $20,000 in carrying costs, and the $25,000 in closing costs and sales commissions, and you've made $75,000 in profit. Imagine doing this over and over again, and you'll understand why many people invest their money in value-added properties!

Create Your Plan

As you consider working with value-added properties, ask yourself: Do I have what it takes to be successful at it?

The answer to that depends on how well you know your own marketplace. Can you sense what people will want and how much they will be willing to pay for it? Do you know something about construction and repair costs? Do you have the knowledge to distinguish a good project from a bad one?

Are you reasonably well organized? Being successful at adding value to property requires good planning and careful thought. You'll have to lay out a plan, pay close attention to details, and keep track of the progress of your undertaking. You can do it yourself, hire someone, or even find a partner to do it for you.

Gary bought five properties in the San Gabriel Valley in Southern California. He paid $520,000 for a four-bedroom, two-bath property and spent another $90,000 in interest fees and upgrades. For more than three months he tried to sell it for $795,000. Although he dropped the price twice, by a total of $70,000, he told me that he was starting to get nervous about it and would be happy to sell it at breakeven.

Before you start investing in value-added properties you should sit down and create a specific plan for what you want the outcome of your investment to be. As you did when you were deciding whether or not real estate investment is for you, you need to decide where you'd like to be in five to fifteen years, how much money you want to invest, how much money you want to make and by when, and what you're willing to do to get that result.

There is one other major decision you have to make before you begin working with value-added properties:

One: Do you want to "fix and then flip" immediately? Doing so will give you the quickest money in the short run, but then you must go out and repeat the process again and again to continue to make money.

Every time you finish a project and sell it, you will be out of business and will have to start all over again.

Two: Do you want to "fix up and hold," rent the property, and let the tenant pay for it? Once your properties are paid for, you'll have rental income for the rest of your life. You'll also be creating wealth through appreciation.

> ### *Tip from the Coach:*
> ### *The magic is in the mix.*

You can also be the one to find fixers and instead of fixing them up, sell the contract to an investor. Your profit will be less, but then so is the amount of time you spend on each deal. The goal is to get the cash register to ring as many times as possible. Several times I have flipped properties before I even closed escrow.

At my company, Dynamics Capital Group, we offer three types of investments: short-term (one to three years), mid-term (four to seven years), and long-term (eight-plus years). My strategy is to flip some, hold some for a few years, and hold some for a long period. It all depends on the properties, the market, and the area. I have found that the magic is in the mix.

Build Your Team

Before I buy a value-added property in any area or state, I build a team to ensure that the work will be done professionally, with care and quality in mind.

Keep in mind that real estate is one of the great cooperative ventures. You need everybody pulling together. People often believe that real estate is a passive activity: Don't believe it! CPAs sometimes call real estate income "passive" income, but somebody has to do the work! (Although it doesn't necessarily have to be you.)

Your team should consist of a CPA, a banker, a broker, a lawyer, a property manager, an appraiser, and a property inspector as well as sub-contractors (a plumber, carpenter, electrician, plasterer, roofer, heating and air conditioning professional, etc). I only use professional contractors who will get the job done right the first time. In the long run, it's always cheaper to use expert professionals, good mechanics, or skilled tradesmen.

My mode of acquisition is relatively simple and straightforward. When I receive a call, I immediately go myself or send one of my trusted associates to see the property. I take about thirty minutes to walk through it with a checklist, noting all the different types of repairs that might be necessary. I estimate the repair costs on the spot. Years of experience have made me pretty good at that! But I no longer do the final inspection myself; instead, I send a professional property inspecttor. My time is much too valuable and is better spent elsewhere.

Choose the *Right* Property

With all my purchases, I try to meet two important investment criteria:

1. A low down payment (a maximum of 20 to 40 percent).
2. And, unless I'm planning to flip it immediately, the property must generate positive cash flow within six months to a year from the date of purchase.

In most markets you can find cheap properties in C or D areas that are in dire need of repair because of neglect or abuse. You can purchase these distressed properties inexpensively at a fair market discount price because of their condition. You can often restore them to their original condition or even better with very little investment. You can sell them a little below market and still generate generous profits. Almost always there is a big demand for a well-maintained property slightly below market value.

Know your market. I have worked in many different neighborhoods and know those markets very well. I can quickly estimate what the property will sell for after the repairs are completed. When I am uncertain of the final market price, I will call on other professionals, including brokers, appraisers, and property managers, who are more familiar with the area or block. Most of them are on my team.

The estimate of the final sales price and the estimate of repair and improvement costs are two of the three calculations I must know before

I make an offer on any property. The cost to carry the property during the period between purchase and resale is the third unknown. With those three costs in hand, I know what I should bid for the property. The deal has to make sense. In other words, I have to pencil these deals out; it's the only way to know if it will work.

How much does it cost to hold a property for six months? A lot. There is interest on the loan, property taxes, and insurance that must be paid while you own it. There is also gardening, cleaning, and upkeep of the property. When you're making your calculations, don't forget the lender's points, the transfer fee that must be paid at the sale of the property, broker fees, leasing fees, title costs, and miscellaneous additional items such as a survey, termite report, appraisal, and insurance. Utilities during ownership can also be expensive.

Tip from the Coach:

The three things you must know before making an offer on a value-added property:

1. Final sales price
2. Repair/improvement costs
3. Cost of carrying the property

Calculate a Property's *True Cost*

Let me give you an example. A typical property might cost me $100,000 to buy. My inspection result is an estimate of $20,000 to repair and fix it up. Now my investment is $120,000. I generally borrow the full cost of purchase plus fixing costs from one of the two or three lenders with whom I work regularly. They will lend the entire cost of the project for no more than 180 days, including the carrying costs, provided the total amount of the loan does not exceed 60 to 65 percent of the future value of the property after renovation.

I personally guarantee the loan and give them a security interest in the property. The total calculation of project costs of one of my projects might look something like this:

Purchase Price	$100,000
Upgrade Costs	$20,000
Total Hard Cost	$120,000
Interest on Loan (6 months at 12%)	$9,375
Lender's Points	$2,500
Real Property Taxes	$2,500
Broker's Fees	$7,420
Transfer Tax	$600
Title Charges	$625
Survey, Appraisal, Insurance	$3,000
Utilities	$3,000
Total Holding Costs	$29,020
Total Project Costs	$149,020

If I can sell the property for $190,000 by the end of the six-month holding period, this will be an attractive project for me.

When I calculate my likely total project cost, I know how much to offer to buy the property and how much flexibility I have to negotiate with the seller. I don't buy in the glamorous areas or historic properties that are featured in so many newspapers and magazines. I like to work in middle class, upper blue collar, or B or C+ areas. I concentrate on particular neighborhoods and look for special properties that have been neglected, but not too badly, and can be resold after repairs and fix ups at good profit. Of course, I don't discriminate against race, gender, or nationality.

Remember that whenever you obtain financing directly from the seller, it's very important to have at least seven years (preferably ten or more) that is an assumable loan or is seller financed. Additionally, when you, in turn, sell the building you can command a higher price if you offer attractive financing and a reasonable down payment.

When you learn to acquire underperforming properties, such as the Mar Vista apartment building I talk about on the next page, you'll also be on your way to earning your first million and thereby achieving financial independence.

A few years ago I bought a fourteen-unit apartment building in Mar Vista in West Los Angeles. The owner was in his early eighties, owned the property free and clear, and was tired of managing it. His son was in his fifties and did not want to take care of the building—he was only interested in pocketing the rent. The rent was 20 percent below market, and there was a lot of deferred maintenance inside and out. Needless to say, the quality of the tenants left a lot to be desired.

There were ten one-bedroom units. Average rent was $750, although the market rent for similar (though well maintained) properties in the neighborhood was $900. There were also four two-bedroom units with an average rent of $920, though the market rent for similar properties in the neighborhood was $1,100. It was a perfect opportunity for adding value. We bought the building at eight times its gross income, or:

10 x $750 = $7,500 and 4 x $920 = $3,680
$11,180 a month x 12 months = $134,000
$134,000 x 8.0 (gross multiplier) = $1,070,000

We put down $150,000, and the seller carried the balance at 7 percent interest for fifteen years. There were no points, loan fees, or prepayment penalties. We spent $70,000 in eighteen months on improvements to the facade, landscaping, painting, lighting, floor coverings, blinds, and fixing the second-floor deck. We brought the income to $160,000 a year then sold the building for ten times the gross income, or $1,600,000, with a gross profit of $530,000 less the $70,000 for improvements and $90,000 in carrying costs, sales commissions, and closing costs. Our net profit was $370,000.

The Benefits of Capital Improvements

Another benefit of upgrading a rental property, also known as making "capital improvements," is that you then have the right to increase rents, which is another reason for purchasing value-added properties. However, to attain the biggest profit, you must document everything.

In some places, depending upon the improvements, you can raise rents as much as 28 percent, if you document carefully. But there are limits to capitalized rent increases. In Santa Monica, for example, a capitalized rate increase is generally limited to about 16 percent. More typical is a 10 to 15 percent increase, meaning that if you spend $1,000 you can raise rents by $100 or $150. That increase is evenly divided among the building's tenants.

In these cases, the raises in rent bypass rent control, which only applies in cities with rent control laws, such as New York or Los Angeles. In other words, a city's Rent Stabilization Board (or other comparable agency) *must* authorize the raise in rents, as long as you document the money you spent on the capital improvements.

In 1998 I bought an eighty-four unit apartment near downtown Los Angeles. The building was rundown and mismanaged. The property supervisor met with the tenants and told them what improvements were planned for the building as well as inside the units. The supervisor explained that we would increase rents modestly and that we expect all tenants to pay rent on time and in full. The supervisor also asked the tenants to respect the quiet enjoyment of the other tenants in the building and to take care of the grounds and the building, otherwise they would have the choice to move out. We would provide $1,000 to anyone who wished to move somewhere else. Surprisingly, most of the tenants stayed; only a few volunteered to leave.

Let's say you buy a property, an apartment building, and you rehab it. Now it's time to raise the rents. The first step is to let the tenants know what you plan to do. That's a good time to also ask them what they would like you to do to improve the building.

Using good customer relations, you ask them, "How can we make your stay with us more enjoyable?" Next, you let them know what you've done to improve the property—especially those things they may not notice, including any work on the air conditioning, roof, plumbing, or heating.

When asked for their opinions, all of the tenants in buildings I have owned have told us that no landlord had ever asked them what needed to be done to their living space in order to make their lives better. But in my buildings, our tenant relations are the envy of other investors. Yes, I sometimes run into difficult people. But out of ten thousand tenants, about ten or fifteen create problems.

Your tenants will appreciate your courtesy, they'll enjoy the building, and they'll work *with* you. Most of all, they'll take care of the building, not because you simply increased the rent, but because you're letting them know that a better living environment goes along with the increase.

To Sell or to Hold?

Giving away hard-earned profits is not good business, so you must make plans to avoid it. There is a time to sell and a time to hold. Cash flow is what allows you to hold on until it's the right time to sell. That's why I always preach that the two most important words in real estate investment are "cash flow."

Proper timing is very important for making big money in real estate. It's like the surfboarder waiting to catch the big wave, what I call selling during an up cycle. Because it's not always easy to predict or to be sure how long a cycle will last, cash flow is important.

Depending on the market and the neighborhood, your fixer-upper could sell as quickly as three weeks or stay on the market for as long as six months or more. The ideal is to have it sold when you are working on it, or even sometimes before you start working on it.

Lack of cash flow is the biggest problem I have with trying to mix investing with speculation. Speculators are often all too willing to tolerate short-term difficulties, such as little or no cash flow, in the hope that they will soon strike it rich from a big sale. Sometimes they do make that big sale—if they time the market properly. But more often than not, the big sale never happens and the speculators lose their shirts.

Financing Your Fixer-Upper

If you don't have enough cash on hand to purchase the property and pay for the repairs, and most of us don't, you will have to determine an appropriate financing option. OPM (Other People's Money) is an excellent option, or you can always contact us at Dynamics Capital. In that case, we'll either buy the property from you or partner with you. If you can find the property and are willing to do the work, we can find you the money. If you have the money and are looking to invest in a fixer-upper, we can help with that too. (Read more about OPM and other investment finance options in Chapter Ten.)

One of my friends has a son who is a lawyer. The son bought a house in Los Angeles from the bank for $175,000. He was very happy. He expected to put in about $20,000 in improvements and sell it quickly at a profit. But when he looked further, he discovered second and third trust deeds, plus tax assessments that were due. The total of the liens on the house equaled $900,000. By foreclosing on the house, they could wipe some of those liens, but in reality everything cost him very close to the saleable value of the home. He did not do his homework before he bought, and it turns out it wasn't such a great deal after all.

Avoiding Pitfalls

Value-added properties are the most sought after real estate purchases, but they can sometimes turn into a headache rather than an equity building vehicle. It's true you can make a lot of money by investing in value-added properties. Yet why are many investors not profiting?

Beware the Gurus. When you look at their investment strategy, it's no surprise some investors are failing. Many people have been brainwashed by so-called real estate investment gurus, the ones who tell you to give them a few hundred, or even thousands, of your hard-earned money and *then* they'll tell you the secrets to making millions fast.

Don't get me wrong. I encourage people to go to seminars, buy books, and listen to audio products. You might learn one or two ideas that will work in your market.

David is a bright, hard-working young man. He has a reasonably good job, but has heard and watched people make money in real estate, so he attended a two-day seminar and spent thousands on books and tapes. He started putting in 25-30 hours a week on his first real estate deal in addition to his regular job. Within two months, he found what he thought was a good property. After he closed escrow it took him two weeks to find out what needed to be done to it.

Two weeks after getting several bids, David chose a contractor to come in and totally renovate the property for $55,000. That included landscaping, paint, carpet, blinds, appliances, and a new wall to close an open area into an additional bedroom. Once the contract was signed, the contractor promised to start renovations in two weeks.

Finally, six weeks later, the contractor started with a bang. That lasted two days; then the contractor disappeared for two weeks. It took David and the contractor eight months to complete the job. David then listed the property with a real estate agent. He did not get an offer for two months, so he dropped the price several times. Finally he found a buyer. Originally, David estimated he would make a $70,000 profit. He ended up losing $62,000.

Often, the gurus will tell you that you don't need a job, money, or credit. All you need to do is pay them, and they'll show you the exact way to make money fast in real estate. Well, I have some bad news for you. Very few of those so-called gurus know what they're talking about, and very few give you a system that is practical and really works in today's market.

They'll tell you that you can even make money at the closing. You make an arrangement with an appraiser and the seller. You inflate the price and get back more money than the down payment, even some cash in your pocket. I don't like this idea, but many people are doing it. However, be careful—lenders, government agencies, even title companies are closely scrutinizing these kinds of transactions.

Some real estate gurus will even tell you that you can buy property way below market with no money down. People buy their books, get very enthusiastic, hit the road quickly, then become frustrated and give up. Yes, once in a while, you can find fixer-uppers with no money down, but it depends on the area and the timing.

Let me ask you this: If you owned a property and you didn't want it anymore, would you give it to someone with no money down at half the price? Or would you instead put it on the market at a slight discount and get multiple offers?

Beware the Rising Cost of Renovations. Keep in mind that over the past few years, the cost of renovating has increased 20 to 40 percent. Plus, when credit is tight and mortgages difficult to get, working with value added properties could get still tougher. A few years back, you could do quite well as the market shot up. However, there is danger in buying and renovating properties when the market is dropping fast

Pierrot bought a small apartment building in Long Beach, California. The cost to rehab it was 50 percent higher than he estimated. But because Pierrot intends to keep the building long-term, he'll be able to regain his money.

To assess the risk you have to understand what you're getting into. How much can you improve the property and still get your money back *and* make a profit?

This is the most critical aspect of making money with value-added properties: determining how a property's purchase price and cost of repairs will play into its resale value under current market conditions. You don't want to over-improve the property for the neighborhood. Be realistic about the financial undertaking as well. No matter who you are and how carefully you plan, it always takes longer and costs more to do the work. And every month that goes by can cost you a lot of money.

Don't Buy at Inflated Prices. I've heard this called "the greater fool theory"—you buy a property at any price hoping another fool will buy it at a higher price. Your deal should always make sound financial sense.

The Time Is Right—Right Now!

No matter how volatile the real estate market may seem, the time is always right to invest in value-added properties. Cities and towns across America are often vastly different, but they're the same in one respect: They all contain mismanaged properties. And that's where *smart investors* can make huge profits in real estate.

Even in a market downturn real estate is a good bet, because it's still one of the safest investments to make in the United States. As the U.S. population continues to grow, more and more people will need housing. Furthermore, real estate has historically increased in value over time. There are fluctuations in the market, including periodic downtrends, but the real estate market always recovers, and property values continue to rise.

> *Tip from the Coach:*
>
> *To succeed in real estate,*
> *one requires only the initiative to start*
> *and the determination to keep applying*
> *the three Rs of real estate:*
> *Renovating, Refinancing, and Reinvesting.*

One of the best aspects and advantages of real estate investing is the leverage gained through the power of appreciation. When you invest in a property that you have decided to lease to a tenant, it actually becomes more valuable, because you don't have to pay the monthly mortgage. Your renter is doing that for you. You're gaining equity in the property without having to put additional money into your investment.

Additionally, inflation affects real estate values. The *rate* of inflation may slow down, but there is always some kind of inflation, meaning that prices will always go higher and your real estate investments will always increase in value.

Moreover, there are many tax advantages to investing in real estate. Income tax laws offer a stunning incentive to invest in fixer-uppers. The interest on mortgage payments can be deducted on your primary residence, and therefore you will pay less in taxes. Real estate investors can also realize additional tax advantages, such as write-offs, depreciation, and expenses.

Faster write-offs, investment tax credits, and the possibility of preservation easement donations greatly enhance the after-tax benefits of ownership that you can use yourself or share with partners or investtors. Additional incentives, provided by government agencies at every level and sometimes by private groups, make value added properties even more profitable.

Although opportunities are much greater during boom times, I have come to the conclusion that opportunities are always present, whether times are good or bad. In bad times you just have to work a little harder, because the opportunities are far and few between. In fact, over the years I've learned that good opportunities never disappear; people simply fail to recognize them.

I believe anyone who really wants to can make a fortune in real estate. To succeed one requires only the initiative to start and the determination to keep applying the three Rs of real estate: Renovating, Refinancing, and Reinvesting.

CHAPTER SEVEN

FLIPPING THE "FIXER-UPPER"

*H*ow many of you would like to be part of the 71 percent of U.S. millionaires who have made their millions in real estate, as we mentioned in Chapter One? I have written this book because I have a strong desire to help others achieve that same kind of financial freedom.

Fixing and flipping properties is a common technique utilized by many millionaire real estate investors, because it can earn big profits *relatively* fast. But it's not an avenue to get rich quickly, and it's not for everyone. In fact, it involves a lot of hard work.

What exactly is flipping? To put it simply: Flipping is investing in value-added properties, and doing it (in real estate terms) at lightning speed. The aim is to add value and then sell as quickly as possible at a substantial profit.

However, in order for you to realize a return on your investment, you must consider location, price, management, timing, and trend; they must all work together to create value.

Karim's Twelve Steps to Successful Flipping

The key to flipping is to follow a system that works. The market is continually changing, meaning that your investment strategies must sometimes be adapted, but there are some principles you should *always* follow when fixing and flipping.

These include:

1. **Find the Right Deal**. There are plenty of deals even in a soft market. Sure they are few and far between and take a lot of work to find, but they are there; you can always find a bargain property

from a motivated seller who has to sell for one reason or another. Learn your market so you can recognize a good deal immediately.

Alfred, who is one of the many people I have mentored, makes three offers every day. Once he finds a good buy or a motivated seller, he assigns his rights to a third party, who pays him a finder's fee. He works hard, but he makes a lot of money.

2. **Establish a Bottom-line Budget Before You Start**. Your total job-cost estimate should be within 5 percent of the total fix-up cost. (Refer to my example, "The Cost of The Property" in Chapter Six.) Be careful: About 80 percent of the time, your actual cost will be higher than your initial budget.

3. **Negotiate the Purchase**. This is where many people run away from real estate. Use your skills or hire someone who has these skills to help you negotiate. (You can read more about negotiation techniques in Chapter Eleven.) Keep your offer clear and simple, and make sure you include escape clauses. A way out should be written into the contract in case something goes wrong. Such clauses include items such as "subject to satisfactory appraisal," "approval of books and records," "approval of physical inspection," etc. (See Chapter Nine for more about contracts and offers.)

Bret is another person I have coached. In his offers, he puts an escape clause, "Subject to my partner's approval," so he can cancel the contract and blame it on his partner, if necessary.

4. **Find Your Money**. It's really much simpler than you might imagine, if you have a good deal. You can use private lenders (hard money lenders), conventional lenders, or investors. You can always contact us at Dynamics Capital. (Read more about real estate

financing in Chapter Ten).

5. **Get Your Team in Place**. You should have your team in place before you close escrow.

6. **Hire Only Competent Professionals**. If you don't have the knowledge, experience, and time to do a good job, hire experienced tradesmen and contractors to do it for you.

7. **Set the Work Schedule**. Have all the bids ready to go and schedule the work as soon as you close escrow. If you've done your home-work, you can start the work within three days of closing. I always do. Set a coordinated work schedule to complete the entire job and have some flexibility to account for the unforeseen. Put completion dates in all your contracts and agreements, and hold everyone accountable.

8. **Supervise the Project**. If you don't have the knowledge and time to supervise the job yourself, hire someone competent to do it for you. No matter how good a team you have, make sure they do what they promise and by when. Use a clear, specific work agreement that protects you—and follow up regularly.

9. **Maintain Quality Control**. Have all the completed work inspected to make certain that it has been done in a professional manner and according to building codes.

10. **Plan Your Selling Actions** (while you're buying). Market your property to specific investors; don't just list the property and hope for the best. Immediately upon closing, put a "For Sale by Owner" sign in the front yard so you can start building a buyers' list. If you don't sell while you're doing the fixing, once the job is complete call all the interested parties and invite them to view the property and make offers. You should also send a postcard (I'm very big on postcards) to all the owners in the area. When you do find buyers, make sure they are qualified.

11. (When you do sell) **Close on the Property on Time**.

12. **Stay legal**. Don't use an inflated appraisal, help your buyer create false W2s, write phony credit letters, or prepare any false documents.

> *Tip from the Coach:*
>
> *Hire a competent lawyer to look at agreements in advance.*

I have sold properties during several stages of improvement, a few of them going before I even started the remodeling! Recently I bought a house in Plano, Texas, an upscale community just north of Dallas. It was a fixer-upper, and I was planning on conducting extensive renovations, but as soon as I put the "For Sale" sign on the lawn, I received several offers. I promptly sold the house and was able to turn a good profit from the property before having to invest any money in improvements.

I purchased another house in Carrollton, Texas, adjacent to Plano, and halfway through renovations I received an offer I couldn't refuse and promptly sold that one as well. However, this will only happen if you're *smart* and put that sign out there right away for everyone to see!

Completing a Successful Renovation

In any property overhaul, there are three things that I recommend you keep at the forefront of your mind:

One: Never compromise on quality; don't cut corners and don't do lazy work.

Two: Keep the cost within your budget. If you don't, you're cutting into profit and thus defeating your purpose.

Three: Focus on timing, because it's absolutely crucial. Every step of the way should be planned and remain consistent with your timeline in order to ensure the successful completion of your project.

Additionally, unless you're a contractor, your focus should be on finding the right property, putting the deal together, and managing the renovation. If you manage the overhaul yourself, you'll learn how much a project costs and how long it takes. But as for actually doing the repairs, ask yourself, "Do I have the knowledge, skill, and experience necessary to do a top notch, professional quality job?" Don't try to save money by doing repairs that you're not qualified to do.

I've seen a lot of money wasted by non-qualified people who end up doing a sloppy job. More money is then spent repairing the shoddy work than if the investor had hired a professional in the first place.

Tip from the Coach:

To build a fortune, you must realize that your time is much more valuable than any savings you might realize by doing repairs yourself.

Curb Appeal Comes First!

You know what they say: You only have one chance to make a good first impression. It's true for real estate as well. When I fix a property or an office building, I always start with curb appeal. A property appraiser will tell you that both the look and the maintenance of a building add value to a property. Real estate agents will tell you that when they go to sell a house, the first thing they do is encourage the seller to fix it up.

I know someone who bought a property that he fixed up on the inside, but not the outside. He had a hard time finding a buyer, because people thought the building looked ugly. When I told him to fix up the outside, he had a much better result. Of course, you still have to fix the whole thing, but start with the exterior. If you don't and leave that chipped paint on the trim, I call it "the kiss of death." It pays to apply a cosmetic facelift to the exterior of the property and grounds.

In Pacific Palisades, California, a friend of mine built a house on a 6,000 square-foot lot. It was a beautiful two-story house, nicely landscaped, about 3,200 square feet. Someone bought the property next door and built the maximum he could on the land: 4,700 square feet. There was no garden or land around the house at all.

When the neighbor wanted to sell, he asked almost 50 percent more than my friend was asking for his property, because the neighbor thought by building more square footage, by building a three-story box, he could make money. But he couldn't sell the house at that price. The neighbor ended up selling at much less than what he had asked.

Conversely, the one who did it properly was my friend. His property had good curb appeal and was esthetically pleasing. Even with less square footage, he was able to double the money he had invested.

Start each property renovation with:

1. Cleaning. Give the building and grounds an industrial strength cleaning.
2. Painting. Preferably two to three modern tones.
3. Landscaping. It doesn't have to be expensive, but it should be eye-appealing.
4. Lighting. Choose lighting that enhances the architecture of the building as well as the landscaping.

Additional items that *must* be cleaned, repaired, or replaced when fixing up the exterior of a property are:

1. Walkways and parking areas.
2. Mailboxes.
3. Exterior doors.
4. Windows.
5. Gutters and downspouts.

6. Roof.
7. Foundation. Have a professional inspect the foundation and structure.

Other small investments that pay big include adding (or replacing) new benches, a birdhouse, a carport or garage, new doorknobs, fencing, a gazebo, new light fixtures, new rocks or wood chips on outdoor paths, sheds, new wood stain on the deck, and new trees or bushes.

Create Pristine Interiors!

Depending on the fixer-upper and the area, there are many potential improvements worth doing. These include adding a master bedroom, a bath, new doors, upgrading the kitchen with modern closets, colors, and appliances, and new showers or bathtubs.

But make sure you don't spend more than you should. My objective is that for every dollar spent I should get $2.50 to $3.00 in return. Don't be cheap; use good materials that last. Just don't overdo it. The bottom line is to be sure that everything you do returns about three times the money you spend.

That means you can't get carried away during the fix-up and spend money on foolish things like putting up *expensive* vertical blinds, carpets, and other floor coverings when the area doesn't justify it. When doing a fixer-upper, never lose sight of your objectives. Stay within budget and buy materials appropriate for the class of property you are upgrading.

For example, for some properties you will flip, it's okay to use vinyl on the kitchen floors. Conversely, for properties that you are not going to flip, installing vinyl rarely is affordable. The labor involved is often three times the cost of the materials. When vinyl rips or tears, it can be expensive to keep replacing. In that case, you can reduce your costs by installing commercial grade tile in the kitchen. If a tile breaks, all you have to do is replace the tile.

Items that *must* be cleaned, repaired, or replaced when fixing up the interior of a property are:

1. Interior doors.
2. Interior lighting.

3. Kitchen cabinets and appliances.
4. Bathrooms.
5. Plumbing fixtures.
6. Heating and cooling systems.
7. Floor coverings.
8. Interior paint.

Other small investments that pay big include new blinds, door-knobs, faucets, shiny new switch covers, and shelves.

Additionally, be careful about asbestos, lead paint, mold, and other environmental hazards.

Hiring a Contractor

Most of the time, due to time constraints, your own skill level, or simply due to the overall size of the project, you will not want to undertake a renovation project on your own. That means you'll need to hire a professional contractor.

Stephaney tried to save money by hiring a general contractor without a license. Due to a dispute, her project was delayed seven months. She ended up paying almost double what she had originally budgeted.

Here are three ways to avoid being ripped off by unscrupulous repairmen, tradesmen, and contractors who make a living taking real estate investors to the cleaners on a regular basis:

1. Hire only qualified, properly licensed and insured repairmen, tradesmen, and contractors. Check references carefully and thoroughly: Also talk to their associates: property owners, contractors, vendors, and employees.
2. Require clear and specific written estimates for every job, including starting and completion dates.

3. Require that each repairman, tradesman, and contractor sign a waver and a release of lien upon final payment stating that they have been paid in full for all labor and materials used on the property.

Check the quality of the materials and workmanship. In addition, make lists of any discrepancies you find and give them to each applicable contractor, tradesman, or repairman to correct. Be fair and realistic, but don't let anyone take advantage of you.

> ### *Tip from the Coach:*
>
> ***Prior to making any final payment to repairmen, tradesmen, and contractors, do a walk-through inspection of the property to determine that all work has been satisfactorily completed—and get a signed release from each.***

Financing Your Flip

Let's say you buy a place for $50,000; you calculate that the market value will be $120,000 when you're finished. You figure you'll have to put $20,000 into the property for improvements and other costs, and you'll hold the property for 180 days. To finance that venture, you're looking at a hard-money loan at a much higher interest rate. In other words, some investor is going to make a lot of money out of your $50,000 profit, so you'll actually make about $40,000 if you hold the property for ninety days. That's the classic flip.

If you find the right property and you know the right people, you can finance your flip with private money, which will cost you $6,000 to $10,000 for ninety days. There are investors out there who would love to be partners with you. (Read more about real estate financing in Chapter Ten.)

Ralph has netted more than $1 million in the value-added market, which designates him as a fixer-upper expert.

"I've done well," says Ralph, who just completed his thirty-second fixer, "but I haven't made money on all of them. Anybody who thinks they are going to make a fortune on fixers and doesn't have the know-how may be mistaken."

Ralph worked in my property management division for more than ten years. He has done more projects than most people and has faced all kinds of challenges.

"If you want to find the right property," he says, "get ready to look high and low for a long time. Be aware of the value and make decisions immediately. Most good deals get bought up quickly."

Working with fixer-uppers is not without its pitfalls. Ralph lost nearly $18,000 on his first two fixers, which would have knocked many people out of the game. He decided he needed a new strategy before tackling his third. I worked with him on a plan and a budget and made sure he stuck to it.

The cosmetic fixer was Ralph's next venture. Just carpet, paint, kitchen counters, and vinyl, and he thought the property would net $28,000 profit. He was off and running. It was like hitting the lottery after two losers. "We only owned the property for six weeks and sold it. Everything worked like clockwork."

However, everything has not been the proverbial "peaches and cream" for Ralph. He has fought for zoning changes, had many challenges with lenders, was on the brink of foreclosure twice, and learned the hard way about IRS redemption periods.

Just the same, Ralph was careful when selecting a competent team and has worked with several of them on most of his properties. Partnering with hardworking, dependable contractors and good real estate agents has been key to his success.

The Reality? It Can Take a *Lot* of Time

Many people who start to invest in real estate don't think about all the time and energy it takes. Keep in mind that fixing and flipping is hard work and takes a great deal of your time. The last time I did any flipping was in California, when my company made ninety-seven offers. To make that many offers, we had to look at about five hundred buildings—before we ever bought one. At that point we realized it wasn't worth it anymore. That's why I elected to purchase properties in other states.

CHAPTER EIGHT

FORECLOSURES

*U*ndeniably, a negative connotation arises in most people's minds when you mention investment in foreclosures. They picture you taking advantage of people who are facing challenges and setbacks in their lives.

That scenario could not be further from the truth. I have bought several properties in foreclosure—land, single-family housing, multi-family housing, and commercial buildings—and I have never been the cause of any of the hardships that the sellers were facing. In fact, as long as you deal with people in a humane way, you are often actually helping by offering them money, giving them a way to get out of debt, and saving their credit, provided they have equity in their property.

Tip from the Coach:

When you buy a house in foreclosure, you're helping people by giving them a way to get out of debt and save their credit.

I like to invest in foreclosures, because that's the time when investors have the greatest chance for buying wholesale-priced real estate. That's also when most sellers are motivated to sell fast. There are wonderful bargains to be found among foreclosed properties—*if* you know where to look and how to deal with them.

When owners cannot or will not make their mortgage payment, they are highly motivated to sell the property, hoping to recoup any equity they may have and save their credit rating. At this time, property owners will at least listen to any offer you make.

> ### *Tip from the Coach:*
>
> ***Look for properties in the first stage, when the owners are having difficulty making payments. Usually they will be more motivated to sell.***

What exactly is a foreclosure? It is the legal means by which a lender may, upon delinquency or non-payment of a mortgage debt by the borrowers, legally seize a property according to the terms of the note, secured by the trust deed. The lender then has the right to sell the real estate and keep *all* of the proceeds, even when there is substantial value above and beyond the debt. The profit gained is not always just monetary. Any personal property left behind with the real estate goes to the new owner as well.

Foreclosure laws differ from state to state, but overall the process remains the same in most of the country. Typically, when properties first appear in the commercial databases (indicating that the owner has received a notice of default), the borrower still has options, including working out a payment plan with the lender or selling the property to pay off the debt.

Essentially, there are three steps in the foreclosure process:

1. The owner cannot or will not make payments for whatever reason, and the lender puts the mortgage in default.
2. After a legally determined period of time, the property is sold to the highest bidder, most often on the courthouse steps.
3. Almost always, the lender is the highest bidder. The lender then takes control of the property and attempts to resell it as a Real Estate Owned (REO) property.

If the problem isn't resolved, the property is put up for auction. But buying at auction can be risky, in part because buyers typically must have cash in hand, can't back out of the sale, have little or no information about the physical condition of the property, and no guarantee that the title to the property is clear.

If the property doesn't change hands at auction, the lender generally turns it over to a real estate broker specializing in the sale of bank-owned properties. The question then becomes: Who is going to clean up the yard and make the necessary repairs before putting the property back on the market? That's often where the investor comes in, buys the property, completes the repairs, and sells it.

In effect, there are five periods during which you can intervene in the foreclosure process to try to obtain your foreclosure bargain. These occur:

1. **Pre-foreclosure**. My favorite way of finding bargains is pre-foreclosure, before a notice of default is filed. This is the time when the owners are already showing signs of financial difficulties. They are one or two payments late on the mortgage, are having difficulties paying credit cards and other bills on time, and are reducing expenditures on luxury items. At this time there is usually very little competition; sometimes I'm the only one talking to the seller.

2. **After the notice of default is filed**. Because the notice of default is of public record, everyone has access to the information, so at this point you'll face a lot of competition.

3. **At the sales auction on the courthouse steps**. Many times, my clients and I have bought very good buys at auction. In each case, we did our homework and knew what we were doing. Investors must be careful since they are not buying the property but rather the lender's position, meaning that there could be other liens and obligations against the property.

4. **During the redemption period**. At this time, the owner of the property can reinstate the loan by making the past due payments plus interest and legal fees. If the lender accepts partial payment— that stops the foreclosure.

5. **After the lender forecloses**. Generally, lenders don't want to own or manage real estate (REO properties); they don't want to have bad loans on their books. That means they may be motivated to sell these problem properties to you, the investor, at bargain prices. All

they want is for you to pay on time and take care of the property.

What Causes Foreclosure?

There have always been and always will be foreclosures. It is simply a part of owning property. As long as there are people experiencing ups and downs in their lives, and as long as there are cycles in real estate, there will be people who are unable to pay their mortgages and who therefore must face foreclosure.

Peter bought a fifteen-unit apartment building in Panorama City, California. On paper the property had a nice cash flow, but Peter didn't do his homework or consult with a qualified professional. For a few months he received less than half the expected rents. This was clearly unacceptable, so Peter went in person to the property to learn what was going on. He was greeted by an armed man who informed him that he didn't want to know what was going on and that he had better leave the building—pronto! Peter was rightly intimidated. He left, never went back, and eventually lost the building to foreclosure.

In a strong market, one would think there would be no properties in foreclosure. Unfortunately, that's not true. The foreclosure rate in good times may be much smaller than in bad times, but foreclosures still occur frequently, even in a strong economy. There will always be owners in the process of losing their properties. In most cases, the causes are:

❖ The owner has over-borrowed and cannot make the payments.
❖ There is an illness, death, or divorce in the family, and no one is available or willing to maintain the property. It therefore becomes distressed and eventually falls into foreclosure.
❖ The owner lost a job or moved and listed the property, but the real estate agent was terrible and no buyers were found. Now the seller, from a distance, will not or cannot deal with the

property any longer.
* The property is in a tough neighborhood, and the seller simply does not care about the property anymore.

The Risks

New—and sometimes even experienced—investors don't always fully understand the risks involved with foreclosure investing. During the years before the 2007-08 subprime crisis, the real estate business was booming, meaning that most bad deals turned out okay as investors were continually saved by historically high appreciation. The years following that crisis have been different, meaning that anything but perfectly executed deals can easily turn bad.

Tip from the Coach:

In most cases, foreclosure properties are problem properties. When you buy them, you're taking on those problems.

Not all foreclosed properties are good deals. The fact that someone is trying to get rid of a distressed property does not automatically make it a bargain. Foreclosure properties in most cases are problem properties. When you buy them, you're taking on those problems, which include (but are not limited to) deferred maintenance, destruction, neglect, high taxes, and high vacancy rates.

Foreclosed properties exist because the owners were having problems. Sometimes the problem is with the property itself: toxic substances that are too expensive to clean, structural damage, the quality of construction, an obsolete location, issues with the foundation, lack of potential income, etc.

Be careful not to let someone else's problems become yours. Moreover, be careful when you buy an REO with a tenant still living in it. It can be very expensive to get rid of the tenant, and you might run into problems that were hidden by the tenant's furniture.

Carlos thought he had found a great buy in Simi Valley, California, on a house located in a very nice part of town. He bought the second trust deed for fifty cents on the dollar. However, he didn't realize the current value of the home was 20 percent less than the first loan on the property—which meant his purchase was worthless. There were also tax and construction liens he didn't factor in. He didn't take my advice—and he lost all his money.

It has been estimated that as many as two-thirds of all foreclosed REOs are distressed, and some are simply hopeless. If you're looking at distressed properties, it's important to determine which have possibilities and which do not.

Remember: The lender will not give you any disclosures regarding the property. REOs are most often sold "as is," even if the lender has already refurbished it. The lender/seller makes no commitment to you of any kind, which can result in severe problems.

In other words, foreclosure properties require time, money, and effort in order to make a profit, so you should buy the property at enough of a discount to make it worthwhile, at least 25 to 40 percent below market value. When it comes time to resell, properties are typically priced at or just below market value.

The costs you must account for when buying a foreclosure include:

- Back payments and penalties.
- Legal costs.
- Back taxes and assessments.
- Repairs.
- Preparing the property for occupancy or sale.
- Lender costs to acquire a new loan or, if possible, to assume the existing loan(s).

Find Those Foreclosure Deals!

How you find foreclosure deals depends on where you are located. For example, in Los Angeles, sources include newspapers (mainstream, such as the Los Angeles *Daily News*, and specialty, such as the Los Angeles *Daily Commerce*), classified ads in newspapers or on the Internet through professional associations, such as the Multiple Listing Service (MLS).

When you find an ad in the paper or on the Internet, look for specific phrases that will let you know the owner is having financial difficulty or that the seller wants a quick turnaround: "desperate," "estate sale," "low down payment," "make an offer," "motivated seller," "must sell," or "take over payments."

Banks, credit unions, mortgage brokers, and private lenders (hard money lenders) can give you information about foreclosed properties. Receivers and executors of wills and trusts are also good sources, as are attorneys and CPAs. Additionally, be sure to keep your contacts open with appraisers, property inspectors, and property managers.

The Internet. There are hundreds of foreclosure websites that keep track of properties. Browsing comes at no cost, but there is often a monthly fee of $40 to $50 to gain complete access.

In addition, the federal government operates its own site:

www. homesales.gov

Visiting the government site is free. It provides information about foreclosed properties being sold by the U.S. departments of Housing and Urban Development (HUD), Veterans Affairs (VA), and Agriculture (USDA).

As a comparison study, I checked www.homesales.gov against three for-profit alternatives for listings in a specific area:

❖ www.realtytrac.com
❖ www.foreclosure.com
❖ www.foreclosures.com

In addition to examining the information each website provided regarding the listings, I talked to real-estate brokers who specialize in foreclosed properties.

Doing so confirmed what I already knew: Novices should approach the foreclosure process and corresponding websites with care. Critics indicate that websites selling foreclosure listings often contain outdated information or listings for houses that aren't ready for sale. Some try to direct would-be buyers to partners with whom they have a financial relationship or to seminars and other products.

Personally, I have run into a lot of problems with foreclosure websites; a lot of the houses can't be sold because the various legal requirements haven't been met, or because the lender hasn't readied the property for sale. What's the bottom line? No matter which website you visit, be careful and go over all the information provided with a cynical eye. Here are some others to try:

- ❖ www.all-foreclosure.com
- ❖ www.catalisthomes.com
- ❖ www.defaultresearch.com
- ❖ www.firstpreston.com
- ❖ www.foreclosurenet.net
- ❖ www.foreclosureradar.com
- ❖ www.homepath.com
- ❖ www.hud.gov
- ❖ www.hudhomesnow.com
- ❖ www.neorealestate.com
- ❖ www.realtystore.com
- ❖ www.realestateforeclosures.net
- ❖ www.reonetwork.com

For Sale by Owner. One way to find properties in foreclosure is to look for "For Sale by Owner" (FSBO) signs. Sometimes people decide to forego the traditional listing process and dispose of the property on their own, or they may have listed a property, but the listing expired with no result. Now, facing foreclosure, the owner is at a final desperate stage. Typically the efforts of such sellers are not productive and may be done half-heartedly as the date of foreclosure approaches. In many cases the only effort may be the "For Sale by Owner" sign in the front yard.

One way to find these properties is to begin touring an area where you're interested in investing (after you've done your homework on the neighborhood). Chances are you'll run across a "For Sale by Owner" sign. Stop, introduce yourself, and talk to the sellers.

The owners are often trying to sell the property themselves in order to save the broker commission. Frequently, they cannot sell and will eventually list the property with a broker. If you've done your homework and know that the property is in foreclosure, you know you've got a motivated seller.

Real Estate Agents. Another source of foreclosure information is via real estate agents. Agents will know if any of their sellers are in foreclosure. Of course, most agents will attempt to buy the property themselves or give it to a friend, which is why you should build good relationships with some agents so you'll be the first to know.

Title Companies. Title insurance and trust companies are good sources of information about recent foreclosures, especially in states that use trust deed foreclosures. (Most states use trust deeds as their preferred lending device. Currently, only ten states still use mortgages.)

Distressed Mansions. The stereotype is that foreclosures don't happen in the best neighborhoods. In truth, they occur in every price range. Foreclosures on high-end homes happen in about the same proportion as they do on other homes. When foreclosures rise overall, so do the high-end ones. In Silicon Valley near San Francisco, the number of homes in foreclosure valued at $1 million or above rose from only one posting in a year to sixteen in the following twelve months during a downtrend in the market.

My friend Alan bought a 7,700-square-foot lakefront Las Vegas vacation home with five bedrooms, a pool, and a waterfall in the backyard. But the best part of all was the price: At $1 million, the house cost $600,000 less than the previous owner had paid three years before in one of the country's hottest real estate markets. Alan bought his new luxury home in a foreclosure sale. He then had to spend $150,000 to upgrade the old carpet, worn tile floors, and an out-of-date kitchen.

Foreclosures can mean some surprisingly good bargains on high-end homes, primarily because banks don't want to be in the real estate business and therefore price their properties to move fast. In Calistoga, California, I have seen a bank asking $1 million for a six-bedroom house that sold three years before for $2.6 million. In Fort Worth, Texas, a bank lowered the price of a 7,700-square-foot home to $1.1

million, down from the bank's original asking price of $1.5 million.

Susan and Larry bought their new luxury dream home by a lake near Austin, Texas, in a foreclosure sale. They paid $500,000 less than the owner had paid for it eighteen months earlier. Larry told me that buying a home this way was much easier than going through a regular sale, since he didn't have to haggle over price or move-in dates with the seller.

Of course, there are drawbacks to buying a house that came on the market due to hardship. In some situations, former owners are bitter and sabotage the house, removing appliances and fixtures. I have found holes punched in the walls of million dollar homes and concrete poured down the toilet.

In other cases, financially strapped owners have allowed the home to fall into disrepair. The foreclosure process typically takes about four months, meaning the grass is often left uncut and the pool looks like a slimy green pond. It wouldn't be unusual to discover that the six-bedroom home you unexpectedly found on the market for $1 million in Calistoga, California, has no insulation—and termites.

Purchasing the Note. In California it takes almost four months to foreclose on a property on a trust deed sale. During this time, the bank not only loses the interest on its loan but will incur many other expenses. Often, lenders are happy to sell the note at a substantial discount because it saves them time and money.

My friend's son thought he had made a killing when he bought the note on a house in Encino, California, for $465,000. But when he found out about the second and third loans and tax liens, he discovered the total debt on the property was $875,000. At the time he bought it, the home was worth $700,000.

I have bought several foreclosure properties at a good price by purchasing the notes directly from the bank or other lenders before or during the foreclosure process and then completing the foreclosure myself.

The Note vs. the Deed of Trust

A loan is evidenced by a promissory note, which means the borrowers are promising to pay back what they borrowed with the terms spelled out clearly: the amounts of principal and interest, the payment schedule, and due dates. Notes are not recorded. The evidence of the note is the deed of trust, which is recorded with the county clerk's office. It shows that the lender has security interest in the property, i.e., the property becomes collateral that will be used if the borrower fails to pay the note as promised.

Approaching the Seller

Now that you have compiled your list of properties in foreclosure, how do you approach the owners? It's easy; call or visit them and tell them you're an investor looking for properties in the area. Ask them if they'd like to sell their house. Tell them you aren't trying to list their house, but are a serious buyer and you're willing to offer them a fair price. Find out if there's a way to make a deal you would both be comfortable with, which will benefit all parties involved.

Sarah and Bill owned a house in Reseda, California, but after they had a major disagreement, Bill moved out. Sarah couldn't afford the house on her own. One of my assistants discovered Sarah had received a notice of default and that she didn't have much equity in the property. Normally I don't buy houses like that, but I felt sorry for her. I gave Sarah $5,000 for the house plus $500 for moving expenses.

Do *not* mention to an owner that you know they're in foreclosure.

Eventually you'll explain to them that you can help them save their credit, and if they have equity in their property, they can also get some money from the sale. Some people will be nasty. Simply ignore them and move on. Others will be friendly, and you'll enjoy working with them.

It's cases like this that help combat the negative associations that people have regarding buying foreclosure properties. With a little tact and persistence, dealing with the owner before foreclosure is completed can be very rewarding. It's also one of the best ways to find bargain properties. In other words, there *is* a way to both help people and make a significant profit in real estate!

I bought a house from Ted in Playa del Rey, California. Ted lost his job and was moving to Florida. Although he had more than $50,000 in equity, he was happy to take $11,000 and move out instead of having to face foreclosure.

In addition to the price you offer, you must account for back payments, fees, penalties, back taxes, assessments, liens, and other costs. Can you assume the loan? How much equity does the seller have in the property? Knowing these facts and figures will help you determine whether the purchase is worth pursuing.

Pre-foreclosures and Buying "Subject To"

Many homeowners are contacted before the foreclosure auction occurs with offers to buy their home. In fact, entire websites are dedicated to updated "pre-foreclosure" lists, which provide not only the name and address of these homeowners, but key details about their property and loan. These sites often hold out the promise of making big profits, even if the investor has little or no capital.

Another way to find pre-foreclosures is through your local County Recorder's office. A deed of trust has a public record, although the loan note does not. Anyone can go to a county courthouse and look up foreclosure notices. There are subscriber services in some counties that will inform you of new foreclosures as they are recorded. You then can try to contact the owners about buying their home, pre-foreclosure.

Most pre-foreclosure investors count on buying property "subject to," meaning they are buying the property subject to existing liens and encumbrances. In plain English that means they are keeping the homeowner's existing loan without taking any formal responsibility for it.

For the investor, the upside to this strategy is that only enough capital is needed to pay the homeowners a small amount for their equity and make the payments until the home is sold. That means that if the investors make a mistake and can't sell the property, they can walk away without any risk to their credit. This is a situation for the seller to beware: While they wait for a sale, unscrupulous investors may never or rarely make payments, further damaging the homeowner's credit while the investors pocket the rental income.

For the homeowners, the upside is that investors buying "subject to" are often willing to pay more. When you're facing foreclosure, it can seem like a world of difference between getting $20,000 rather than $10,000.

Of course, homeowners facing this decision should carefully consider the risks. Selling a home "subject to" transfers control of the homeowners' credit to the investor. In other words, other than coming up with the cash to pay for a home they no longer own, there is nothing the homeowners can do to regain control over their credit.

If the investor keeps the property as a rental and regularly pays late or misses payments to the mortgage, that history will be reflected on the seller's credit. This situation can continue for the length of the loan, perhaps up to thirty years. Homeowners are often better off letting the property go to auction, because that at least starts the clock on the foreclosure disappearing from their credit report (which currently takes seven years).

Tracy had a house in Hawthorne, California, in which she had about $45,000 in equity. She lost her job and was in default on her home loan. Troy offered her $3,500 to move out and said he would take care of the house, but he never paid the mortgage or the taxes. Tracy not only lost the house, but also ruined her credit.

There is some risk for investors as well. Most home loans have a "due on sale" clause, meaning that the loan can be called due in full upon sale of the property. A case could be made that concealing the sale by not paying off the loan is fraud. However, most lenders are happy to continue getting payments so they don't have a bad loan on the books.

The Trustee's Sale

Trustee's sales, also known as foreclosure auctions, *should* come with a big sign that says "Buyer Beware," but they don't. That means that you must be very careful if you're going to show up to bid. Before you get there, you should already know what liens and encumbrances there are against the property you intend to buy.

Keep in mind that the buyer has the right, as long as the note does not contain a balloon payment, to bring the loan current until five calendar days before the date of the trustee sale. And within those five days before the sale date, if the beneficiaries (lenders) want to reinstate the borrower or accept payment in full, they can.

> *Tip from the Coach:*
>
> *Foreclosure auctions should come with a big sign that says "Buyer Beware" —but they don't.*

Furthermore, sometimes the lender will postpone the auction without giving a reason. In fact, lenders can change the date and place of a trustee's sale in order to discourage other buyers, and they sometimes do so repeatedly. Their motivation, of course, is to get the property as cheaply as possible. Lenders also usually have a list of known and trusted investors whom they inform about the auction before anyone else.

Sometimes you only know when you're actually at the steps of the courthouse that the sale has been delayed. If the sale is postponed, the borrower still owns the property.

Finally, if you want to go to an auction to buy property in foreclosure, don't do it alone. Take a professional; if you don't, you can lose your shirt pretty quickly.

Title Insurance and Property Profiles

As you're preparing to purchase your foreclosure property, you will want to get a profile of the property that tells you about all the liens and encumbrances against it. You can obtain three levels of information about property from title companies: a property profile, a preliminary title report, or a title report. The latter comes with the purchase of a title insurance policy.

Keep in mind that simple property profiles are notoriously unreliable. They are not guaranteed and are by and large assembled by the lowest paid people at the title company—who don't always care what they're doing. The simple profiles contain only easily available information, probably just the recorded deeds of trust against the property and the tax liens.

A preliminary title report should show you everything that will eventually show up on a full title report, although there are some exceptions. However, you'll only get free preliminary reports a handful of times before a title company will stop giving them to you.

We put twenty fourplexes under contract plus nearby land to build an additional twenty. The preliminary title report was clean, but a survey showed two easements in the middle of the land, one twelve feet wide and one twenty feet wide. That meant we could only build eight more buildings. When we asked the title company why the easements didn't show up on the preliminary title report, they responded, "That's why it's called a 'preliminary' title report." Needless to say, we had to cancel the agreement and lost quite a bit of money.

Smart real estate investors will spend the money and pay the title company to give them accurate information, which means purchasing title insurance and a title report. That will get you accurate, detailed, and guaranteed information. The amount of the insurance you carry should be in proportion to the purchase price of the property.

> ### Tip from the Coach:
>
> **A smart real estate investor will spend the money for title insurance in order to gain accurate, detailed, and guaranteed information about the title and all the liens on a property.**

You can also find additional information about a property, such as brokers' price opinions, which are available on the Internet. Plus if you want a general feel for how many clouds are on the property title, it's public information, obtainable through the county recorder's office for a small fee.

If you want to know if taxes are delinquent, however, you'll have to dig a little deeper or wait for the title report. You will not see supplemental taxes on a simple property profile, although you will likely find out about the general property taxes.

If you're buying property in an established neighborhood, and it's a single family residence, title problems, other than taxes and some utility easements, are not typical. Finding out that a property has a forty-five-foot easement, for example, usually happens only with a commercial development.

When you get the title report, in addition to the history of the property and succession of ownership, the items that you will be looking for are:

- ❖ Deeds of Trust
- ❖ Liens
- ❖ Tax Assessments (including supplemental assessments)

❖ Easements
❖ Notices of Default

The items will be listed on the title report in their priority of succession. That is, there is seniority to the liens. For example, California is a "race" state in which the first person or entity to file a lien on a property has seniority, meaning that all other liens below it are subordinate, except for taxes and construction. In fact, it's possible to have a smaller first trust deed and a larger second, and even a larger third, considering the way people were putting extra loans on their property as equity increased rapidly before the subprime crisis.

Let's say a deed of trust has secured an original indebtedness of $348,000. The next items you may see are taxes, which are always senior to the deed of trust. Additionally, any construction done on a building that creates a lien has priority over the first loan, provided the construction started before the first loan was recorded.

Let's say you have purchased the note on the property and you find out that yours is Loan No. 3 in succession. What happens if Loan No. 3 is delinquent, but Loan No. 1 and Loan No. 2 are fine? You may be foreclosing, but you are subject to the first two liens that are senior to yours. That means you will have to keep the other loans current.

Additionally, if you are purchasing a foreclosure and see a Notice of Default filed on the property, there will be back payments due. And keep in mind that you are not privy to the note, which tells you the interest rate.

The Due on Sale Clause

Most notes and deeds of trust have a "due on sale" clause. The reason it is included is that when banks lend you money on a property, they know you. They have run a credit report, and they know who you are. They don't want somebody they don't know to step into your shoes and automatically become their borrower, because they might not know anything about that person.

Do banks typically exercise the due on sale clause? Generally, no, but sometimes they do. Once a loan has gone into default, bank regulators will require the lender to increase the amount of it reserves to cover the amount of the loan in default, meaning that the bank now has a bad loan on its books and will have less money to invest elsewhere. The reasoning behind the practice goes back to the mid 1980s, when banks were carrying a lot of bad loans.

REO Properties

Real Estate Owned (REO) is a term used to describe a property repossessed by the lender after foreclosure. The more property a bank has in its portfolio, the more motivated it will be to give you a good deal.

> *Tip from the Coach:*
>
> *Dig your well before you're thirsty: If you want good REO referrals, start building relationships with lenders now.*

REOs provide very good business if you have a contact at the bank who will let you know before a property is offered elsewhere. That makes it doubly important to build relationships with lenders. In other words, dig your well *before* you're thirsty.

In the current credit market, bank regulators are stringently looking over the shoulders of the banks to make sure that they meet standards, dispose of bad loans, and avoid making bad loans in the first place whenever possible.

Lenders have a set point where they can comfortably keep a certain number of REO properties in their portfolio without a problem. But when those numbers increase, bank officers become edgy, which means your potential increases for getting a bargain on one of these properties.

The first REO bargains you'll see will occur mostly with single family homes. Income properties will be the last to become available from lenders, because most have enough income to cover expenses, especially when rents and occupancy rates are high. Of course, when vacancy rates are high, that can change.

Short Sales

A short sale occurs when a homeowner sells a mortgaged property for less than the outstanding balance of the loan and turns over the proceeds to the lender. In other words, the lender agrees to accept less than what is owed, which means you, the buyer, will pay less. Most lenders will accept less than the full balance of the loan plus fees when purchased by a third party, but historically they have not accepted less than what is owed to reinstate a borrower in default.

If the owner has no equity, you as the investor can work on the short sale directly with the lender. The first step is to sign a purchase agreement with the seller contingent upon the lender's acceptance of a short sale. Next, you must get permission to negotiate with the lender on behalf of the seller.

Each lender has certain rules and guidelines to deal with a short sale, so make sure you learn and follow them. Keep in mind that lenders are very busy, so it can take 60-120 days before the bank makes a decision to approve a short sale.

When you contact the lender, make sure you speak to the person in the work out department who can make a decision, not the loan servicing officer. Write down the entire conversation and keep a copy of everything you send them for your records. Respond promptly to their calls and provide them with whatever information they require.

Be professional. Don't tell them about how much it will cost them to foreclose. Instead, just be willing and able to close fast once a decision is made. Remember that you're buying the property in "as is" condition. Don't ask for special conditions and don't play games.

Did you know you can also negotiate short sales on other liens and seller's debts? These include judgments, tax liens, mechanic liens, and personal debt.

Avoiding Pitfalls

Do Your Due Diligence. To avoid the worst pitfalls in foreclosure purchases, do your due diligence. Know everything you can about the property in which you are investing. With HUD foreclosures, and even for other foreclosures, you must be careful. Sometimes neither the

HUD official nor the real estate agent has inspected the property from the inside. I once went to see a house where nothing was left except the main door and the studs. Everything else was gone. I couldn't even locate the kitchen or the bathrooms, because there were no closets and no fixtures.

Close Before You Pay. Never pay the seller or the lender before you close escrow. Furthermore, never pay the seller any money directly. Put the money in escrow and make sure that you have the title insurance and the deed of trust before you release the money.

Never Rent to the Seller or sell the property back to the owners who were just in foreclosure. They have already demonstrated that they either may not or cannot pay their bills.

Get a Title Insurance Policy.

Record the Trust Deed Promptly.

In the early 1980s, I bought a house in the early states of foreclosure from Barbara in Westchester, California, near Loyola Marymount University. I gave her money and failed to record the transaction right away. In the meantime, I rented the property out to someone, only to discover that Barbara had also sold the property to someone else. As it turned out, Barbara sold the property to five different people! That taught me to always record the documents promptly.

Watch Out for Inflated Home Appraisals. When the housing market cools, buyers must confront a problem that was easy to ignore during boom times: inflated home value appraisals. Critics inside and outside the appraisal business have long warned that many appraisals are unrealistically high. That, in part, is because generous appraisals help loan officers and mortgage brokers, who often choose the appraiser. If a home appraises at less than the buyer offered, the deal is likely to fall through.

Inflated appraisals didn't matter much when home prices were rising at double-digit rates, because market values would quickly catch up. However, when prices level off or fall rapidly, some investors have found that the actual market value is below what past appraisals led them to believe.

Lenders and government agencies are trying hard to crack down on these practices. Unfortunately, they are not able to catch all of them.

Foreclosure DOs and DON'Ts

Here are a few DOs and DON'Ts to follow as you pursue foreclosure investments:

* ❖ Do make offers on properties in areas you know well.
* ❖ Do check the preliminary title report.
* ❖ Do check for toxics, chemicals, etc.
* ❖ Do check the zoning on raw land.
* ❖ Do check to see if improvements meet zoning permit requirements.
* ❖ Do visit the property and look for signs of gangs in the area.
* ❖ Do check the property survey (boundary, easements, etc.).
* ❖ Do check with local police for the crime rate in the surrounding neighborhood.
* ❖ Do check sales comps in the area. A friendly real estate agent can help you, or you can go to www.realtor.com, where the MLS (Multiple Listing Service) information will help you estimate the property value.
* ❖ Do check with a lawyer to understand what the sellers' rights are. Do the sellers have the right of rescission? If yes, the process could take few days or a few months.
* ❖ Do make sure all the people on the title sign on the sale.
* ❖ Do make sure you have a clear title with no liens, including second or third trust deeds, mechanics liens, or tax liens.
* ❖ Don't skimp: Pay for a title insurance policy.
* ❖ Don't make just a verbal agreement. It's not worth the paper it's written on.

CHAPTER NINE

OFFERS, LETTERS OF INTENT, AND CONTRACTS

*B*y the time you're ready to make your first offer on an investment property, you should have already set down your goals and done the prep work. Let's say you're now an expert in the market in which you want to purchase. You've decided what type of property is appropriate for your interests, and you've found a property that interests you.

The next step is to make an offer. But just as important as making a *good* offer is actually taking *action* to make the offer. Many people new to the real estate investment business make the mistake of sitting back and waiting far too long—until they learn *everything*—before they make an offer on a piece of property. Make the offer, and then learn as you go. The best way to learn is by doing.

Tip from the Coach:

Motivated sellers are excellent sources of bargain properties. You can often buy at a reduced purchase price and often with attractive terms.

Know Your Sellers' Motivation

One of the most important steps in the process of making your offer is to pre-screen your sellers. In doing so, you'll save yourself a lot of time, expense, and hassle. Make sure up front that you can make a good deal with a seller. You also must ensure that the deal works well for you financially.

Of course, the process is easiest if you buy from sellers who tend not to care. Those kinds of people are the owners of seized and foreclosed-on properties, corporations, nonprofits, and uninterested heirs as well as other disinterested parties, such as probate attorneys, and properties you obtain through tax sales and private auctions. These sellers are often highly motivated to get a property off their hands quickly.

But no matter who you're dealing with, you'll want to know as much as possible about the sellers and their motivation. Make sure you ask about everything that has to do with the property, why they're selling, and what they want to do with the money.

Gather as much information as possible. Asking the following questions will help you know what kind of offer to make as you're negotiating with the sellers:

- Are you the owner? Are there other people involved in the decision-making?
- Why are you selling? What do you want to accomplish?
- How long have you owned the property?
- How long has it been for sale?
- What improvements have you made since you bought it, and when were they completed?
- What kinds of people live in the area?
- Tell me about the advantages of this particular property.
- What about the disadvantages, if any?
- What kind of problems have you faced since you bought the property?
- Are there loans on the property? How many? What are the balances?
- Do you need all cash, or will you consider carrying some paper?
- What will you do if the property doesn't sell?

Making Lowball Offers

Once you've pre-screened the property and your seller and you're looking to make an offer, make sure it's a reasonable one for all concerned. Don't insult your potential sellers with a horribly low offer; you'll simply turn them off to working with you. By the same token, ensure that working a deal with them will ultimately make you money. You're in business to make money, not to be a free service to someone.

First, as an investor you seldom want to pay the asking price, unless an uninformed seller is asking well below market, which happens only occasionally. Sellers almost always ask more than they're willing to accept for their properties. They expect to come down some, hence the above-market asking price. If you pay what the seller is asking, you're wasting your money. Remember: The less you pay for the property, the greater your profit when you sell.

Yet, as you're determining what to offer, keep in mind that price is not *always* the most important thing. Many times I *have* paid full asking price, but with other terms that made the deal worthwhile. At other times I paid full price, and a few weeks later received an offer $100,000 to $300,000 more than I paid, because I knew I was getting a bargain.

In other words, when I see a good deal, I buy it, because I *know* it's a good deal. The fact that the seller is asking a certain price doesn't mean that I should always negotiate for less. That can only happen if you know your market.

Try offering 15 percent less than what you intend to pay. You never know; the sellers may accept it. If they don't, you still have that 15 percent in which to negotiate, and you'll still be at or below the price you originally had in mind.

If the sellers' final counter-offer is higher than the mark you've set, walk away. But leave your latest offer on the table, meaning that it still stands. Don't deposit earnest money, but leave the paperwork. The sellers may stew on the offer and call you a month later to accept the deal.

The real trick is in knowing how much less than the asking price a seller will take. Sometimes a seller will only come down a few thousand dollars. Other times they may drop 10 percent or more. And, of course, there's that occasional seller who will refuse to come down a dime.

How do you know one from the other? That's why you should do your homework and know as much as you can about the sellers' motivation. For example, if the sellers counter your offer at a discount of 5 percent of the asking price or more, that means they are motivated.

Give the Sellers What They Need

The key to getting what you want is to give the sellers what they need. The trick is discovering what they need, and if it's not what they're asking, to make them aware of it.

For example, a seller might think he wants a $50,000 down payment from you in order to buy a boat. In reality he doesn't need the $50,000—he needs the boat! Can you be creative and work out a way to get him the boat without having to come up with $50,000 for a down payment?

A few years ago one of my clients (Peter) owned a townhouse in Marina del Rey, California. He wanted to sell it and live on a boat on a lake in Colorado. Another client (Steve) owned a boat in the Marina and wanted to buy a condo or townhouse to live in and conduct his business. I put the two together, and now they both have what they want, with very little money exchanged.

Karim's K.I.S.S. Rule

"Let me see if I understand your offer," said the nervous property owner. *"You want to buy my property using a double-crank, triple-wrap, nothing-down, cash-back-at-closing technique you learned at a get-rich-quick seminar . . . because it will be best for me?"*

Frequently I see rookies and sometimes seasoned investors make complicated (and what they *think* are creative) offers that confuse sellers and make them suspicious. I have seen offers that contain every power clause and secret phrase and technique there is. Let me ask you: What would you do if you received that kind of offer? I don't know about you, but that sneaky kind of proposition would make me run in the opposite direction.

My advice is to instead use my **K.I.S.S. Rule: "Keep It Short and Simple."** (I bet you thought the phrase might involve the word *stupid*, but I want to avoid that word when talking about offers.) At the same time keep your offer clear and specific. In making my offers, I only use words and phrases that are easily understood by the sellers.

I have been the most successful by using simple, everyday language. I explain clearly what I want and why—and because I do that, sellers often gladly accept my offer.

Writing the Offer

In your written offer, make sure you specify who will pay for what, including the title company, escrow, surveys, homeowner warranties, appraisals, termite inspection and eradication, repairs, and making the unit(s) move-in ready.

There should also be contingencies in the offer for negative situations that arise from the inspection of books and records, from a thorough physical inspection, and in case of termites or toxic substances as well as a contingency that takes into consideration your ability to obtain reasonable financing.

Additionally, unless the seller is carrying the mortgage, make sure you qualify for a loan at reasonable terms. However, if you can and are willing to buy a property for cash, call me right away. My contact information is at the back of the book.

In summary, make your offer easy to understand. Get the option to buy, but use contingencies to protect yourself.

Not long ago, there was a small office building for sale on Sawtelle Boulevard, north of Olympic Boulevard in West Los Angeles. The owner was an older doctor who wanted to retire and move to the desert. He received many offers. He told me that although my offer was not the highest, he decided to accept it, because I was straightforward with him and made a very simple offer.

The Letter of Intent

The letter of intent does not constitute a binding contract, but is intended to be used to tell the seller the exact terms of your offer. It's used at the beginning of the process of purchasing a property that interests you. Once it's signed, it will tie up the property for a couple of weeks, giving you a head start to do your homework and begin collecting the necessary funds to close the deal.

If you're ready to make an offer and have it accepted, your Letter of Intent must be drawn up. It should consist of certain minimum content, which includes:

Sample Letter of Intent

This is a **Letter of Intent** to purchase the 136,000 sq. ft. Heartland Shopping Mall located at 300 Early Blvd., Los Angeles.

Our offer:

Purchase Price of $10,250,000, including 2% commission to Dynamics Capital Group.

Down payment is $3,075,000.

This offer is subject to the buyer acquiring a loan of $7,175,000, amortized over 30 years, at a maximum interest rate of 6.5%.

The title will be taken by Karim Jaude, and/or nominees.

This Letter of Intent is subject to inspection and approval by the buyers, within 30 days from the date the final contract is signed, and on receipt of a copy of the leases, and other documents necessary for the due diligence.

The closing will be within 60 days of the removal of the physical, and books and records contingencies. Buyer has the option to extend closing for an additional 15 days if lenders require it to close.

Buyer has the right to re-inspect the property within 3 days prior to closing.

Buyers to deposit in escrow the amount of $100,000, with "_____."

Title Company shall be "_____."

Once signed, this offer binds both parties, and seller agrees to remove the shopping center from the market.

This offer is valid until _____ 5PM PST.

Should you have questions, please do not hesitate to contact me at 310-555-1234.

I look forward to working with you.

Sincerely, Karim Jaude

- ❖ Addresses and phone numbers of all the parties.
- ❖ Address of the property to be purchased.
- ❖ Purchase price being offered.
- ❖ Down payment being offered.
- ❖ Buyer's contingencies.
- ❖ Name of the person who will take title once the property is sold.
- ❖ Proposed date of closing.
- ❖ Amount of earnest money to be deposited.
- ❖ Escrow company or other party who will hold the deposit.
- ❖ Date the offer expires.
- ❖ Signature and date lines for all parties.

Make sure you have all the terms in the Letter of Intent that are necessary to tie up the property (the sample Letter of Intent on p. 124 shows a typical document except for names, addresses, and signature lines).

As soon as the seller has signed the Letter of Intent, I begin to draft a summary of the investment to show to the investors. I also contact them to see who is liquid and who might be interested in that particular property. Additionally, I contact my due diligence team, so they'll be ready when we finalize the contract.

The Purchase Contract

When it comes time to prepare the contract, be fair, and you'll be richly rewarded. It should go without saying, but you must make sure that the contract is in writing, or it will not be valid.

The elements to be included in the written contract must identify: the buyer and seller, the property with enough specificity so that you can tell what it is that's being purchased, the amount of the purchase price, and when and how the funds will be paid. If you have included all those elements, it's a valid purchase contract.

Unlike the letter of intent, which is basically a non-binding agreement to agree, the contract is binding—if you have the essential elements in writing.

The elements to include in the written contract are:

- ❖ Seller's information.

❖ Buyer's information.
❖ Property information.
❖ Sales price and financing.
❖ Earnest money.
❖ Title Policy and Survey.
❖ Condition of the property.
❖ Closing and possession dates.
❖ Settlement expenses.
❖ Language regarding mediation and arbitration in case of dispute.
❖ Payment of attorney's fees.
❖ Option to terminate.
❖ Additional clauses, as necessary.
❖ Signing details.

Sara had excellent credit and a high net worth. She wanted to buy a shopping center at a bargain price in a great location in the South Bay in Los Angeles County. It was 80 percent occupied with financially strong tenants. There was a clause in the contract stating that she must remove the loan contingency within thirty days from the opening of escrow. Sara told the sellers she wouldn't have any problem getting a loan. She removed the loan contingency two weeks before she was due to close, and suddenly area lenders began changing loan terms at the last minute. Her lender requested that she pay a 45 percent down payment instead of the 27 percent agreed upon a few weeks before—or they would not fund the project.

At that point Sara was faced with a dilemma: She would either lose her $150,000 deposit (and risk getting sued) or be forced to find money at any price. All because she didn't receive the right advice and didn't keep the right clause in the contract to protect her.

Commercial Purchase Contracts

Because of the complexity of most commercial real estate purchases, you must complete a more thorough due diligence as you're working with these properties. As a result, all commercial purchase contracts should contain the following contingencies:

❖ **Satisfactory Physical Inspection**. Make sure you learn about everything that has to do with the physical property, including (but not limited to) the foundation, electrical, environmental issues, deferred maintenance, plumbing, roof, structure, or termites. I always include a clause that will give me the right to reinspect the property within the last three days before close of escrow. You'll be surprised what you sometimes find. I have walked away from many deals because of what was discovered during physical inspections.

❖ **Books and Records**. You should examine all leases, history of occupancy, any concessions being given by the seller, tenant turnover rates, delinquencies, service contracts, warranties, special offers, and agreements.

❖ **Loan Qualification**. Unless the seller will be carrying your mortgage on the property, make sure you are able to find and qualify for a loan at reasonable terms, and include that as a contingency.

A few years ago I put an eighty-eight unit apartment building in Phoenix under contract. The building was supposed to have only three vacancies. During the due diligence period, the inspection showed only three vacancies, but three days before closing there were twenty-two vacancies! There were a few old suits in some of the closets and a sofa or a beaten mattress in the apartments, but no sign of real people living there. When I asked the seller for a discount to reflect the real occupancy, he responded that I was too smart for him, and we agreed to cancel escrow.

Another time, I was buying a 166-unit apartment building in San Antonio. The purchase price was based on 94 percent occupancy. Upon checking the books and records, we discovered that the real collection rate was only 62 percent. Needless to say, the investors and I did not go through with the purchase.

Ten Important Commercial Sales Contract Clauses

When you are examining the purchase contract on a commercial property, make sure that it's fair to you as well as to the seller. Whatever you do, keep it clear, short, and simple. The following clauses should always be included to ensure that you, as the buyer, are protected:

1. **Who Pays for What?** Will you pay the attorney's fees in case of litigation, arbitration, or mediation, or will the sellers? That question should be answered in the contract. Also make sure you know who will pay for title company fees, escrow fees, updated surveys, home owner warranties, appraisals, termite inspection and eradication, making the vacant units move-in ready, and repairs.

   For example, every lender requires an updated survey. If your contract is not clear that the seller must pay for it, you'll be the one paying $3,000–$7,000 out of pocket.

2. **Prorated Contracts**. Make sure that any long-term contract on the property that is signed within one year of the date of purchase is pro-rated for the life of the contract. Such items would include rent concessions, laundry leases, etc.

   A few years ago, I bought a forty-four-unit apartment building in Tarzana, California. Three months before opening escrow, the seller signed a laundry lease for ten years, pocketed $45,000 cash, and accepted 25 percent of the laundry proceeds for the next ten years. During our due diligence, we caught it and were able to require the seller to reduce the price by $42,000.

3. **Prorated Income and Expenses**. The prorating of rents, taxes, assessments, security deposits, etc., should be clear and specific in your contract. Additionally, I always require that the seller provide me with estoppel certificates signed by each tenant at least three days before the close of escrow. The tenants will document in the

certificate that the terms of the lease are correct, as is their security deposit, that they have no claims against the property, and that they have made no outside or special agreements with anyone regarding their unit.

> ### Tip from the Coach:
>
> *As a buyer I like to close escrow on the third or the seventh of the month so the sellers must pay the full month's rent in escrow—whether or not they have collected all the rent. As a seller, I like to close escrow toward the end of the month, so I'll have the whole month to collect the rent.*

4. **Remedies for Damage during Escrow**. The contract should specify what remedies are due the buyer if the property is damaged during escrow due to fire, earthquake, flood, mudslide, tornado, etc. The buyer should have the choice either to continue with the purchase (and receive value for the damage) or to cancel the contract.

A few years ago, I bought a 136-unit apartment building in Dallas. During escrow, a hailstorm damaged the roof. The seller was willing to assign the proceeds from his insurance company to us minus the deductible, but because our contract was clear, we collected the money from the insurance company, and the seller had to pay us the deductible out of pocket.

5. **Legal Notifications**. Immediately after opening escrow, make sure

that the seller notifies you of any code violations on the property, any notices received from the city, fire department, or health department, etc. The seller is responsible to remedy any violations that happen before or during escrow.

I was once buying an office building near LAX airport. During the due diligence period our CPA discovered, in an office drawer, a final notice from the fire department requiring the owners to immediately correct a substantial and dangerous safety violation, which was expected to cost about $2 million. Of course the sellers did not want to tell us about it. Sure, we could have sued them, but who needs the aggravation?

6. **In Case of Default**. If the sellers default, what compensation does the buyer have? If the sellers change their mind, or one of their partners or relatives wants to take the property, they cannot just give you back your escrow deposit. The contract should contain a clause that protects you as the buyer, giving you either a large sum as compensation or giving you recourse to sue the sellers for specific performance. And, of course, there should be a clause to compensate the seller if you as the buyer do not perform, excluding the contingencies written into the contract.

When Scott bought a property, there was a clause in the contract stating that he must inform the seller three days before closing whether he had final loan approval. If he did not inform the seller, he would forfeit the loan contingencies. Scott and his lender both forgot about the clause, and Scott waited until one day before closing to inform the seller that he was not able to acquire a loan. He lost his $100,000 deposit.

I *highly* recommend that you or your lawyer make a schedule from the opening through the closing of escrow of what needs to be done by when as well as what actions must be taken. That way you won't miss a deadline, and you won't lose your shirt.

7. **Personal Property**. During your due diligence, make a list (take an inventory) of all the personal property on site so that you know what you're buying, and include this information in the contract. This includes items such as appliances, light fixtures, etc.

The main entrance of the 204-unit apartment building in Phoenix had sumptuous, high ceilings and a beautiful crystal chandelier. The office was equipped with up-to-date computer systems. When we closed escrow, the computer systems and the chandelier had disappeared! Because the contract was clear and we had completed an inventory during the due diligence, the seller was forced to give them back.

In another deal in San Antonio, the seller took the air conditioning motors located alongside the exterior walls. We were able to make him bring them back, because they were clearly listed in the inventory.

8. **Records**. Make sure that prior to closing the seller is required to deliver all tenant files to you, including applications, late fee records, leases, notices, special events, tenant screening, etc.

More than fifteen years ago I bought a 160-unit apartment building in Aurora, Colorado. When we took over, half the tenant files had somehow disappeared. We had to evict half of the residents, and because of the missing documents it took us more than a year to clean up the building and reconstruct the files of the remaining tenants.

9. **Property Maintenance during Escrow**. Include in the contract a provision stating that the seller must keep the property well maintained and respond to tenant maintenance requests promptly during the escrow period.

When buying a twenty-one-unit apartment building in Palms, we were in escrow for three months. During that time, the seller did not do any repairs and let the building run down. A week before the close of escrow, a tenant called a city inspector, who gave the seller a citation. We were able to delay closing escrow until the seller performed all the city's requirements.

10. **No New Contracts**. Include in your contract a provision so that from the date you sign the Letter of Intent the seller cannot bind the property with any contract beyond the close of escrow without a written agreement from you, the buyer. This includes new tenant leases or lease renewals.

In San Antonio, I purchased a 104-unit apartment building that was 82 percent occupied. During escrow, the seller rented sixteen more units to unqualified tenants, seemingly to anyone who breathed! He didn't care who they were as long as they paid him a lump sum of cash. Because our contract was clear, we were able to delay the closing until the seller evicted all the unqualified tenants.

Keep in mind that if you have a binding contract on real property, you can specifically enforce that contract. In most places, real property is deemed unique. Therefore, monetary damages are not considered sufficient if the seller fails to perform. If you really want the property and the seller backs out or isn't living up to the contract, you can force the selling party to sell you that property—if you have the right contract.

Additionally, in more than forty years of real estate investing, I have learned to only sign a contract that is drafted or reviewed by my lawyer. I never just blindly sign the broker form or the association form. Those forms are drafted to protect the broker and the seller, never the buyer.

Finally, don't try to save a little money by not hiring a competent real estate lawyer, who right away will explain to you the importance of having a good contract in place. The few thousand dollars that you spend on a lawyer will save you tens of thousands—even hundreds of thousands—later, along with headaches and aggravation. A good attorney can help you avoid being sued and, if you *are* sued, can help you avoid losing your shirt.

Twelve Essential Real Estate Forms

You should be able to obtain the following useful and necessary real estate forms from your state's Association of Realtors:

1. Commercial Sales Contract
2. Lease with Option to Buy
3. Letter of Intent
4. Loan Assumption Addendum
5. Loan Documents
6. Notice of Termination
7. Offer
8. Options
9. Property Condition Disclosure
10. Residential Sales Contract
11. Seller Financing Addendum
12. Third Party Financing Addendum

PART IV:
TAKING YOUR SUCCESS
TO THE NEXT LEVEL

CHAPTER TEN

OPM AND THE INCREDIBLE POWER OF LEVERAGE

*Y*ou want to buy an investment property, but you don't have money for a down payment or closing costs. "Well, just forget it!" That's probably what you've been told by people who think they know what they're talking about—but simply do not.

What Is "OPM"?

OPM (Other People's Money) is perhaps one of the greatest secrets of the richest people in the world. The most successful real estate investors tend to use OPM. Moreover, throughout my years of experience I have discovered that OPM is the *best* source of cash for your real estate deals.

> *Tip from the Coach:*
>
> *OPM (Other People's Money) is perhaps one of the greatest secrets of the richest people in the world. It is the **best** source of cash for your real estate deals.*

The more you use other people's money, the faster you'll make your millions. OPM is like a snowball rolling down a steep hill; it grows amazingly fast. The higher the return on the investment, the faster it grows. So I encourage you to start investing with OPM now, because the sooner you let that ball roll, the quicker you'll make your millions.

Mark, one of the people I have mentored, was a real estate invest-ment broker. He was good at finding properties, but didn't have the money, nor could he raise enough, to invest in any. I helped him find an investor, Jerry, who also happens to be a good manager.

I coached both of them to start syndicating apartment buildings. They started part-time. Mark and Jerry were able to build a for-tune, quit their jobs, and are now doing real estate investment full-time. They're making five times more in real estate investments than in their old jobs.

The Incredible Power of Leverage

As we discussed in Chapter One, leverage is simply controlling a lot of real estate with little or no money of your own. The question is not *if* you should leverage, but by how much. How much you should leverage (the ratio of your down payment to your loan) depends on your risk tolerance and your ability to carry the loan in slow times.

What many people don't realize is that when a property appreciates, it does so on the value and not on the original investment. For example, if you put down 20 percent on a property, and the property increases in value by 10 percent, you've just made a 50 percent profit on your money. That's exactly why real estate looks so good to people and why using leverage makes so much sense.

For example, when you buy a property at $200,000 and get a loan for 80 percent of the value, or $160,000, your down payment equals 20 percent, or $40,000. Therefore, if the value of the property increases by 10 percent, or by $20,000, you have earned a 50 percent profit on your money.

Additionally, one of the greatest advantages of real estate investing is the power of leveraging with OPM. If you leverage a property with Other People's Money, you can make an investment even more valuable by renting it out. The monthly mortgage payment is now being paid by the renter, which means that your tenant is paying for your equity growth.

Remember: You want to leverage but not too much. You still want to be able to service the loan. Otherwise, you could create a lot of stress for yourself, and you may even lose your investment.

Obtaining Your Primary Real Estate Loan

Today, everybody borrows to buy real estate, which is virtually the only wide-scale investment made with financing. You can obtain your primary loan (to be used for the bulk of your purchase, apart from the down payment) from traditional sources, which include banks, credit unions, insurance companies, mortgage bankers, mortgage brokers, savings and loans, and thrifts.

The amounts and rates will vary from institution to institution. These lending sources are less expensive, although the cost of your investment money also depends on the location of the property, its condition, its income and expenses, your expertise, and the quality of your credit.

> *Tip from the Coach:*
>
> *When you're financing long-term, you want the lowest interest rate possible. When your objective is to fix and flip quickly, the interest rate isn't as important as the upfront costs, points, and fees.*

Keep in mind that as you put together your deal, you will need to demonstrate to the lender that you can turn your investment property into an income-producing, valuable piece of real estate. Lenders are looking for specific experience with the type of property for which you are securing the loan. The lender wants to be convinced your management skills can turn your project around, and they want to see specific market experience.

In the 1990s, I bought several properties from a bank, because the bank officers knew that I was experienced, had an effective property management team, and could act fast. Whenever they had an apartment building that was not performing, they called me first.

There are lenders out there who are willing to provide financing for income-producing and transitional properties, but they're not doing it foolishly. They are looking very carefully at the people involved. If you're just getting started, there will be no prior projects on your résumé. In that case, then you'll need to partner with the right people who can demonstrate that their other projects have been successful.

The lenders will often want to meet with you and your project manager at the property, and you will need to give the lenders a sense that you can take the project from A to B and complete it successfully. Lenders would also like to see other completed successful projects within a five-mile radius of your subject property. Drive by and show them how the properties are doing now and describe what they used to look like.

Of course, if you know that going the traditional route will not work for you, you can choose instead to use hard money lenders for quick financing. These lenders are more concerned with the property itself and how much equity you will have in it rather than with your credit history. Typically, hard money loans come at a greater cost (higher upfront fees and points as well as a higher interest rate) and occur over a shorter term.

Additionally, there are a number of opportunistic funds available. For example, my company, Dynamics Capital Group, runs a fund that is geared for a quick turnaround.

Jesús was good at finding properties and fixing them up, but he didn't have money. Several times, he came to my company to borrow money for a purchase and for fixing up a property. My company gave him the money and took a share of the properties.

Once you have completed the loan application paperwork, the time it takes to obtain the funds can vary. For traditional financing, the rule of thumb is that forty-five days is a comfortable time frame from the day I submit the application to the day I get the money.

With opportunistic funds, if the answer to your application is a yes, the loan could be completed in two weeks. Keep in mind, however, that there are a lot of reports that need to be completed, including the appraisal, engineering, the Phase I Environmental Assessment, the legal review of the title, the survey, etc., and that all takes time.

If everyone is committed, traditional financing *can* be done inside of forty-five days, sometimes even in thirty days. But don't forget that the shorter the time frame, the more stress it puts on your people to get all the work done.

Finally, when you're shopping for lenders, how do you determine which is the best deal? The answer depends on your objective. When you plan to hold a property for five years or longer, you want to find the lowest interest rate possible, and the best loans have fixed interest rates and are assumable without qualifying. If you're buying the property to flip within three years, then the interest rate is not as important as the upfront costs, points, and fees.

Buying with No Money Down

You've probably heard, read about, and maybe paid for a course teaching how to buy property with no money down. The real estate gurus make it sound easy, give copious testimonials, and show off their flashy materials. The truth is that most of it's a lot of hype.

Sure, you can buy property with no money down, and I've done it myself many times. The question isn't *could* you, but *should* you?

In my experience, it's best to be careful with little-money-down, or no-money-down deals. When you buy a property with no money down, often there's a reason why you are able to buy it that way—and it's often something negative. As I've said before, you don't want somebody else's problem to become your problem. You want to buy a good property that will make you money.

Seventeen Sources of Down Payment Money

1. **Personal Resources**: cash, lines of credit, personal loans, loans on

life insurance policies, credit cards, or retirement accounts, such as an IRA, KEOGH, or SEP.

2. **Friends, Relatives, or Business Associates**. These people should be contacted one-on-one or in a small group, either at offices, a restaurant, a hotel, or community halls.

3. **Joint Ventures**. You can work with an active or silent general partner who raises all or most of the capital for your investment project.

In the early 1980s, I wanted to buy a forty-unit apartment building in Sherman Oaks, California, for which I needed to raise $900,000. Within four weeks of closing, I had only raised $450,000. Instead of panicking, I spoke to everyone I knew and was introduced to Kevin, a semi-retired real estate syndicator.

Kevin liked the property location and the partnership structure and felt comfortable with my ability to manage it effectively, but he did not want to get involved directly. He agreed to help me raise the money in return for a share of the general partnership interest, without being on the records and with no other involvement.

Kevin sent the investment summary to all his investors and gave me their contact information to follow up, which I did. I was able to raise the money and close escrow on time.

4. **Private Equity Funds (Equity Lenders)**. This is also known as equity participation through partnerships. When an individual investor or company provides capital and takes shares of the partnership, it is equity participation, not a loan.

5. **Hard Money Lenders**. Hard money lenders provide unconventional loans that are not provided by an institution. The fees and interest are higher, and in general these have a shorter term than regular loans.

6. **Mezzanine/Bridge Financing**. This kind of financing can be obtained from private investors or institution lenders. When an investment property needs substantial rehab or remodeling or you are converting it to a different use to maximize the return on your

investment, initially there will be no cash flow. Most conventional lenders will not give a loan on a property without enough income to pay the mortgage. However, there are certain lenders that will provide enough cash for a short period as you turn the building around. They are paid *after* the building shows proof of cash flow at which point a conventional loan is obtained.

7. **Centers of Influence**. That is to say, you can seek funds from attorneys, bankers, CPAs, financial planners, or investment advisors; business managers, hedge fund managers, money managers, pension fund managers, or private equity investors; and insurance, real estate, or securities brokers, all of whom will invest or help to raise some or all of the money from their clients, friends, or business associates.

8. **Professional Organizations**. Airline pilots, attorneys, carpenters, CPAs, doctors, electricians, engineers, nurses, writers, as well as city, state, or federal employees often belong to professional organizations and unions in which you can network or have associates network to find sources of capital.

9. **Seminars**. I hold real estate seminars, where potential investors often express an interest in investing. There are a multitude of real estate seminars out there in which to network for investment funds.

10. **Investment Clubs**. These organizations exist all over the country. Investment clubs offer groups or individuals the opportunity to invest in everything from stocks and bonds to commercial or residential real estate.

11. **Seller Financing**. Sometimes the seller will agree to carry the note on the property.

We bought a building in Venice, California, by assuming the first trust deed and securing a second trust deed for $254,000 from the seller, who knew and trusted me and my investors. The seller was willing to advance the money and accept the second position, provided we spent the $254,000 repairing the building. We paid very little money down: only the closing costs. We rehabbed the building and sold it within three years at good profit.

You may also obtain a wrap-around loan from the seller. That is, instead of assuming the first loan from the lender and taking a second loan from the seller, you can have one loan that combines both. You then pay only one monthly payment to the seller; the seller turns around and pays the original lender.

Seller financing is an excellent way to go. In general, when a seller agrees to finance your investment property, you can obtain it with the least down payment and the best interest rate and terms. In addition, there will be no appraisal fees, points, or other fees that come with getting a loan from a traditional financial institution or private lender.

There typically won't be any prepayment penalties, no recourse, and most importantly, the owners will be more flexible. If something goes wrong and you have to delay one or two payments, they are likely to be more understanding. In some cases you'll be able to purchase the property with a very low down payment, or none at all.

12. **Government Insured Loan Mortgage Assumption**. These are government-provided or -guaranteed loans for people who have served in the government or in the military.

13. **Barter**. You can trade one property for another. You may also trade a boat, a car, a plane, an RV, etc., for real property.

14. **Over-Borrow**. If an owner wants to sell a building to someone who doesn't qualify for a new loan, the buyer can purchase subject to the existing loan.

    The buyer will then pay the mortgage directly to the seller, who will in turn pay the lender. The buyer can borrow extra, with no need to qualify with the bank. In that way, the investor buys the property subject to the existing mortgage.

15. **Lease with an Option to Buy**. If you can find interested tenants, they can put down a deposit and sign a lease with an option to buy your property. Some will even be willing to do the property repairs.

16. **Add Repair and Closing Costs.** You can obtain a conventional loan for an amount that includes the sales price, plus repair and closing costs.

    The lender will then give you back the extra money at close of escrow. That way, you pay very little or zero cash out of pocket. The lender then oversees the disbursements as they are used to pay for closing costs and repairs.

When my company bought an apartment building in Glendale, we arranged with the seller to have the cost of repairs included in the sales price. The purchase price was $2,300,000, and we needed $300,000 for repairs, so the sales price was written at $2,600,000. In turn, the seller gave us $300,000 at close of escrow for the repairs. But a word of caution regarding this approach: The building must appraise at the combined figure (in this case, $2,600,000). If it doesn't, the bank won't loan that amount.

17. **Inflate the Price**. It is technically possible to up the sales price and get the extra funds back at close of escrow. But be careful: Many investors have abused this practice, meaning that lenders as well as government agencies are after them. Sometimes the real estate broker and the appraiser plot to report an appraisal at a much higher value than the true value of the property. That practice is fraudulent and is something I would never do myself.

Additionally, some buyers advertise for investors on the Internet, in newspapers, on the radio, and even on television. Others copy the names of investors from records at the county recorder's office or buy a list of investors from list brokers. But be warned: The securities laws are very strict regarding how you can solicit investors. Unless you intend to sponsor a public offering, I would not advise you follow these practices.

Raising and Managing Your Investment Finances

There are things you can do to make it easier to raise the money you need to invest. Depending on the objectives of the investor, if a project offers most or all of the following, it will be easier to raise the capital:

❖ Require a minimum investment of $10,000 to $50,000.
❖ Offer a regular distribution of cash flow to the investors.
❖ Highlight the depreciation and tax benefits.

- ❖ Highlight the potential appreciation.
- ❖ Use the right amount of leverage (down payment): not too high, not too low.
- ❖ Explain the calculated risks.
- ❖ Explain the high potential for return on the investment. But be very careful. The securities laws are very specific about what you can and cannot say, so never guarantee the investment or a specific return.
- ❖ Always strive to deliver more than you promise. If you think you can deliver a 15 percent return, tell the investors they'll get 13 percent. If you deliver half a percent less than what you estimated, the investors won't be happy. But if the return is half a percent or more higher than what you told them, not only will they be pleased, but they'll be much more likely to reinvest with you later on and recommend you to their friends and business associates.
- ❖ Create a mechanism in which investors who need to bail out can do so by selling or borrowing money against their shares. The capital does not have to be returned in full, although the amount should be fair to both the buyer and the seller of the shares. Offering a way out will accelerate your ability to raise capital and help make your investors feel comfortable.

If it becomes necessary to bail out an investor, how do you do it?

- ❖ By using your own money.
- ❖ By making arrangements with other investors who are financially capable of purchasing other investor shares.
- ❖ By raising capital reserves specifically for that purpose.
- ❖ By making an arrangement with the investor's bank to lend money on the shares.

In every partnership I sponsor, I plan for at least one of the above contingencies that allow me to help an investor facing a challenge. Sometimes I have been successful, but a few times I have not. That's why I do not knowingly accept investors who might need their money during the investment holding period.

Next, as you determine how much cash you'll need for your purchase, make sure you also raise enough cash reserves for emergencies.

Don't forget that the two most important words in real estate investing are cash flow. As I've said before, you won't make big money from cash flow alone, but it will help you carry a property during economic downturns. You want to hold onto the property until it has appreciated enough that you'll make a profit. Make sure you have enough income from the property or cash on hand to carry the property, if it becomes necessary to do so.

Additionally, give yourself enough time to raise the capital required —but not too much time. You want to avoid investor procrastination. As you're requesting funds, set a short period. The cut-off date can always be extended by the managing partner. However you *must* set a deadline. And if you don't raise a minimum amount by that date, you should give the money back to the investors.

Finally, as you're raising money for the down payment, closing costs, and repairs, make sure you qualify and are able to acquire a loan to finance the rest of the purchase price, unless the seller is carrying the financing.

Several years ago I wanted to raise $1,500,000 to syndicate an apartment building. I needed $1,300,000 for the down payment, the closing costs, and minor repairs. I wanted to raise an additional $200,000 as a reserve, but three of my investors disagreed. These were seasoned syndicators who had invested half of the capital I needed. They didn't want to give me the additional cash and told me they would give me the money later if I needed it. Two years later, I needed the money, but they didn't pay. I struggled a bit until I was able to borrow the money—at a higher interest rate.

Defining the Roles and Responsibilities of Each Partner

When you take on partners the terms and conditions of the investment agreement should be well thought out, carefully discussed, and agreed upon by all of the partners in advance. As you put together your deal, you must answer and consider the following:

❖ Is the deal fully understood by all the partners?
❖ Will your business entity be an LP (Limited Partnership), GP (General Partnership), TI (Tenants In Common), or LLC (Limited Liability Company)?
❖ Will there be a general partner or a managing partner? How will he or she be compensated?
❖ Which partners will contribute which amounts of money, and when will each payment be due?
❖ Will any of the partners be expected to contribute any additional capital or loans at a later time? By what date?
❖ When will the capital contributions be returned to the partners?
❖ When will cash flow be distributed?
❖ Will there be any reserves? What amount?
❖ Who will manage the property? What powers will they have? What compensation will they receive?
❖ What recourse will there be? That is, when you borrow money from the bank, the bank takes a lien on the property. When the loan allows recourse, if the property drops in value or is destroyed, the bank can go after the investors' other personal and real property. With a no-recourse loan, the only property the bank can go after in case of loss is the property on which it holds a lien.
❖ What if one or more partners want to sell? To whom and at what price will they sell their shares?
❖ How do you determine (and agree on) the value of each partner's interest?
❖ Can you arrange to allow for the assignment of rights to a new buyer, so that you will not have to pay the loan in full when the property is sold?

Avoiding Pitfalls

Avoid Short-term Loans with a Balloon Payment. Be careful—*smart investors* understand that the money market could get tight, making it very expensive to refinance when it comes time to pay a short-term loan with a balloon payment, and the lender can go after your personal property. Also watch out for prepayment penalties, since you don't always know when you'll be selling the property.
Never Sign a Loan with a Recourse Clause. If you do, you'll be

personally responsible for the loan. You don't want to be liable for the loan if something goes wrong with the market or the property. The worst-case scenario without a recourse clause is that you will lose the property, but you will *not* lose your shirt.

(Please note: Did you know that FHA and VA loans can be assumed without qualifying with no points or personal liability, i.e., no recourse?)

Keep Enough Cash Reserves for Emergencies. Remember, the two most important words in real estate investing? *Cash flow*. Leverage will not help you if you lose the building to the lender.

CHAPTER ELEVEN

THE POWER OF NEGOTIATION: HOW TO GET WHAT YOU WANT (AND MORE) BY GIVING PEOPLE WHAT THEY NEED

> *The art of negotiation is practiced by everyone, but the craft of negotiation is practiced by few.*
>
> *—Anonymous*

Karim's Nine Keys to Negotiating the Best Deals Ever

*T*he following nine keys will unlock the door that leads to negotiating the best real estate deals.

1. **Everyone Negotiates.** Be aware that every day we negotiate with our bankers, colleagues, employees, spouses, children—even our pets. We all do it every day over loans, projects, privileges, raises, dinners, dates, even the holiday leftovers. We all negotiate, whether we want to or not. Some of us just do it better than others.

2. **Know What You *and* Your Negotiating Partner Want.** You'll hear me say it again and again: Do yourself a favor. Before you enter into a meeting, take a few minutes to know exactly what you want, what your goals are, what your objectives are, what you would like to achieve from the negotiations, and what outcome you desire. What other options are available to you? The more options

you have, the better the deals you can negotiate.

Next, please do your negotiating partners a favor. Know what *their* objectives are. Learn as much about them as you can: their wants, needs, aspirations, fears, and limitations. What other options are available to them? The negotiations will go more smoothly, and you'll get much better results.

I have a daughter who wanted a new cell phone called the Sidekick, serviced by T-Mobile. We had a contract for another year with Verizon; to cancel would cost $250.

She started by asking me, "Daddy, I'm a very good student, am I not?"

I said, "Yes."

"All year I didn't ask for anything, did I?"

"No."

"I never asked for designer clothes or shoes, did I?"

"No."

"In three months I'll be sixteen, correct? You're going to give me something special when I turn sixteen, aren't you?"

"Yes."

"You don't have to give me a car yet. All I want is a Sidekick, and I want it now."

Friends, with such negotiation skills, I could not say no.

It's your job to find out why the sellers want to or must sell. Have they experienced a personal, financial, or family challenge? Are they moving? Has there been a partnership dispute? Motivated sellers are excellent sources of bargain properties. They have special reasons for wanting to close deals with you, which means you can buy at a reduced purchase price and with attractive terms.

That means looking beyond the other parties' *position* to learn their *interest*. Their position, i.e., the sales price they're asking, only outwardly declares what they want. Their real interest is the motivating need for the sale.

Be sure you know the sellers and their motivation. Ask them a lot of questions to learn as much as you can. Gather as much information as possible. Ask about everything that has to do with the property, why they are selling, and what they want to do with the money.

Paul was in the garment business. He needed to raise capital to buy inventory for his business. His inventory turned over at least four times a year, and as banks tightened credit, Paul was not able to get as much money for his business as he needed.

Paul wanted to sell his property in order to get immediate capital. When I learned that, I told him he could put his building on the market and maybe get a couple hundred thousand more, but it would take him three to four months to sell . . . or he could sell it to me for $200,000 less, and I would close fast. Of course, he sold it to me, and we both won.

Remember in Chapter Nine how we listed questions you should ask the sellers to determine how to make the best offer? Make sure you ask them *at the beginning* of your negotiations. The answers you receive will give you the information you need in order to successfully negotiate the best deal possible.

A few years ago, I was negotiating to buy an industrial building in Ontario, California. After several offers and counter-offers, the owner and I thought we should meet face-to-face at the building to hammer out the final details.

However, when I arrived, the owner himself was not there, only his son and an officer of the company. I chose not to go through with the negotiations. Instead, I arranged a lunch meeting with the owner halfway between Ontario and my Brentwood office on another date. At that lunch, we sealed the deal.

3. **Always Negotiate with the Decision Makers.** Don't negotiate with someone who doesn't have the power to make a final decision. Don't give your final concessions unless you are in front of the decision makers, and don't try to make a deal with someone who doesn't have the final say. Otherwise, you're just wasting your time.

4. **Build a Relationship.** Negotiation, as a highly efficient form of communication, requires trust. Good business and personal relations will make it mutually beneficial. Remember that it's likely that many people with whom you negotiate, you'll met—and negotiate with—again. That's why it's important to build good relationships.

For that reason I advise against trying to squeeze and intimidate incredible terms out of the sellers. That defeats the very purpose of the craft of negotiation. Instead, look for win-win situations in which both parties can work together to solve each other's needs.

Be cooperative with people; we all respond well to positive human contact. For example, when entering into negotiations, I never sit across from the sellers like an opponent. Instead, I sit next to them so we can all look at a white board, on which I list the give-and-take we need to solve the problem.

In 1981, one of my European investors hired a lawyer who went in for the "kill" in a water bottling project (long before bottled water was popular) involving the city of Palm Springs and the local Indian tribes. The lawyer forced their hand to get the most he could. Although my client got his permit, his lawyer alienated all the parties involved.

My client ended up with severe restrictions on what could have been a mutually prosperous water bottling plant. It did not make business sense anymore. Because the lawyer thought only of winning rather than of what would be mutually beneficial, my investor ended up walking away and losing a lot of money.

As it has in many other instances, this relationship-building key came into play when I wanted to purchase a foreclosure property from First Federal Bank. They needed to get a certain price out of an apartment building so they would not lose face with bank regulators. They had already agreed to sell below market price. Although I could have driven harder for an additional $40,000 decrease, I instead put myself in their shoes. Because I played fair, they offered me a loan with lower interest and a lower down payment. That saved me $80,000. It was a win-win deal.

Remember: Good negotiations make repeat performers. First Federal had other problem properties on which they gave me the first right of refusal at below market value. We each got a fair deal, consistently. Together, we negotiated the purchase of fifteen other properties that earned me a half million dollars in profit.

5. **Exercise Patience.** When negotiating, *never* lose your temper and *always* take your time. Whoever negotiates in a hurry will make the most concessions. If you don't have to, don't show your hand openly too soon. Being too open can hurt your negotiations, because you're exposing your cards before the other parties have exposed theirs.

A few years ago, I made an offer on an apartment building in San Antonio, Texas. It was a very good building and was reasonably priced in a great location. Valerie, the broker, was very rude and aggressive. We did not get along at all. However, the deal was so good that I had to put my emotions aside. I called her and said, "You have a building that you want to sell. I'm a serious buyer, but we don't get along. Why don't you have someone in your office work with me on the logistics to close the deal in thirty days?" That way I didn't have to deal with Valerie anymore, and I closed the deal.

Focus on terms instead of people's manias. Wait out their anger, intimidation, impressive jargon, guilt trips, and tendency to "fake it" just to manipulate you. Let the numbers decide—not your emotions or theirs. If the other party won't budge, I can always postpone the negotiations until the next day, or I can walk away.

> *Tip from the Coach:*
>
> *Whoever negotiates in a hurry will make the most concessions.*

Getting angry in a negotiation only closes the doors of communication and impairs your judgment. In a few rare cases, I have been in negotiations with people who have genuinely made me mad. They have been unreasonable, rude, and offensive.

I have sometimes felt like turning the table on its end and storming out the door. I have had to train myself to stay cool in these situations and to keep thinking clearly. If you can stay calm when the other party is angry, you're the one who has the upper hand.

6. **Turn a Conflict into a Conflict Resolution.** Negotiations are not one-time deals or competitions, but a process to work out agreeable terms. Instead of turning a negotiation into a conflict, turn it into a conflict resolution. Watch how non-verbal cues reveal the other parties' interests. Wait for them to make the first move; never negotiate against yourself, by proposing a concession you're willing to make.

Quite often I will start the negotiations with the terms and conditions that are easiest to agree upon and leave the harder ones until later. This style of negotiations worked for Secretary of State Henry Kissinger, when he brought the Arabs and Israelis together in 1974.

Use open-ended questions that stimulate solutions. For example, "Could you help me see what you need to feel good about this?" Listen actively to the others' concerns. What I do is rephrase their important points, add in my own position, ask another question, and then shut up.

Instead of arguing for what you each want, you can settle for what you both realistically need.

7. **Make Concessions in Small, Diminishing Increments.** Most negotiations require each party to make concessions. How you make these concessions is important. I make my counter offers in small increments.

Let's say you're trying to purchase a rental property, and the owner has agreed to carry paper on it. You've agreed on interest rates and all the other elements of the deal. In other words, this is one of those cases that comes down solely to price.

You offer $750,000 and the seller counter offers $795,000. You go back the next day and offer $760,000. The seller doesn't accept the offer and counter offers. The following day you return with an offer of $765,000. While you're waiting, you get nervous, so before hearing back from the seller you offer $767,000.

I contend, however, that it's a bad idea to outbid yourself. I generally don't like to overbid myself (that is, to keep bidding without first receiving counter offers from the seller).

Remember: By making concessions that become incrementally smaller with each offer, and by never overbidding yourself, you're sending a message that says: "Hey, I'm not going to give you too much more, and I am getting close to my limit."

8. **Lose a Few Skirmishes and Win the War.** In your negotiations try to identify one or two points that are relatively unimportant to you, but which seem important to the other parties. Let them win those skirmishes. This will appease the sellers and make them feel that it's their turn to concede a few points. It will also make you look like a good guy who is willing to give a little in order to make a deal.

When my son was younger, he used to ask me for something again and again and again, forcing me to say no, no, no. Finally, with a doleful expression on his face, he would say, "Well can I at least have an ice cream cone?" I would say yes, not realizing that's probably what he wanted in the first place. Sound familiar?

Don't accept the first offer and don't make a concession without asking for something in return. Make sure your initial proposal includes terms you can willingly sacrifice. Negotiate value, but don't go past the lowest price that will allow you to make a meaningful profit.

9. **Be Willing to Walk Away.** Before you walk into a negotiation, set guidelines for when you plan to quit. Don't let your ego or emotions compromise your limits. Too many bidders pay inflated rates at auctions, for example, because their egos take over. They wouldn't walk away from a sale outside their limit.

Not long ago I went to an auction for an office building in Beverly Hills that was in probate. The building was valued at $4.2 million. I set a limit for myself at $3.6 million and stopped when I reached it. The bidding continued with four to five bidders. When the bid reached more than $5 million, just two people continued. They kept outbidding each other until finally one of them bought the building for $7.3 million, $3 million more than what it was worth, all because of nothing more than ego and pride.

If in a negotiation the other parties and I hit a deadlock, I head toward the door, turn, and say: "I'm sorry we can't come to terms. I really want this. You really want that. You also want a fair price for all. I must be doing something wrong." At that point, stop and be silent. Sometimes this tactic works; occasionally it doesn't.

I *never* threaten, "This is my last offer." For most negotiators, it usually isn't, so they just end up making liars of themselves.

Sometimes I may suggest we move to a different setting—get a drink or have lunch or dinner. Then we resume the negotiations from where we left off. But if at that point the other parties try to keep the terms in their favor and try to change *back* the ones in my favor, I say goodbye. I won't tolerate the "oh-I-forgot-about-it" tactic thrown in at the last minute.

Remember: If the deal doesn't make sense, don't be afraid to walk away.

> *Why spend thirty years learning about something through trial and error, when you can learn it in thirty minutes from someone who already knows?*
>
> —*Dr. Ralph Smedley, Founder, Toastmasters International*

Finally, I strongly recommend that if you don't feel comfortable doing the negotiating on your own, seek out the help of a competent professional, a master at the craft of negotiation.

CHAPTER TWELVE

HOW TO KEEP MOST OF YOUR PROFIT: THE TAX ADVANTAGES OF REAL ESTATE INVESTING

I have always believed the adage: There is no "patriotic duty" to maximize your taxes.

Yet because real estate is fixed in place it will always be subject to local taxes, fees, restrictions, and assessments. You won't be able to avoid most of these (there are exceptions), but you should be aware of them *before* you commit any investment funds.

> *The bottom line is this:*
> *Real estate is the most*
> *potentially lucrative*
> *of all investments,*
> *and it is a fantastic tax shelter.*

The primary focus of this chapter is on federal (and some state and local) taxes that apply to the income generated from your real estate investments and how you can plan your investment and business operations to maximize your net return with the taxes in mind.

Here, you'll find out ways to maximize your deductions and credits for local charges—especially for real estate property taxes—that may be generated from your real estate investments in order to also shelter your other income from taxes that might apply.

Managing Real Estate Investing with Taxes in Mind

First, let's start with some background information that will help you to manage your real estate investments with the taxes in mind:

- ❖ Tax planning for real estate is complicated. It is best to bring in tax professionals well-acquainted with real estate. Bring them in early, *before* committing substantial funds to your real estate investment program.

- ❖ Your tax position for real estate investment income will largely depend on the form of entity (business partnership or corporation) that you use to commit funds to the investment. Your choices are many, but the most preferred entities are those that allow pass-through of tax attributes directly to you. Normally, this would be some form of partnership or limited liability company (LLC), but almost never a regular or "C" corporation, which can subject your income to double taxation.

- ❖ Real estate is unique as an investment opportunity, because it has for decades allowed significant leverage (that is, the use of OPM—Other People's Money), generally through borrowing. The costs for those borrowed funds (the interest and fees you pay on borrowed money) are generally deductible from the income from your real estate investment.

- ❖ Cash flow is king in real estate investing. You should always try to invest so that you obtain a positive flow of funds from your investment. Minimizing your tax obligation will help you maximize your cash flow.

- ❖ Real estate is considered a longer term and generally illiquid investment. Therefore, unexpected events should be expected. Always provide a secure source of additional funds to meet these kinds of challenges. One of the key reasons for minimizing and deferring taxes from your real estate operations is to maximize your available capital to finance new and continuing real estate ventures.

It's a Complicated System

If anything is *more* certain than death and taxes, it's that tax laws will change every few years. Sometimes there are even retroactive changes that will affect you a year or two down the road on the investments you are making today.

In fact, tax laws are really a reaction to what happened yesterday. If we've had ten years of incredible returns on real estate and Congress wants to know where they can get some money, they look back and see there's a ton of money available in real estate, so they tax it. If a state government is running a deficit, state officials often decide they'll tax real estate in order make up the deficit.

To be frank, you could spend all your time trying to understand and stay up to date on tax laws alone, or . . . you can listen to an expert. You should *always* seek the services of a qualified accountant or a tax professional to determine how to best plan for yourself and the property you are buying.

Choice of Organization

Although real estate is generally a longer-term investment, your time horizon for investing may vary considerably, meaning that the best choice for your investment vehicle will also vary.

For instance, if you intend to invest short-term income, you may choose to make personal investments in real estate mortgages or trust deeds.

Our focus in terms of reducing taxes, however, is on equity investing in real estate for long-term appreciation. Therefore, your focus here should be on your needs for investments that are short-term (two to three years), medium-term (five to eight years) or long-term (more than eight years). The term refers to how long you intend to hold an interest in the real estate before cashing out your investment.

Generally, the simplest investment vehicle works best for shorter time horizons, while the more sophisticated form is justified for longer term investments. Why? In part because the costs to establish and maintain the property are different depending on how long you hold it, and also in part because the more sophisticated the vehicle the more it can be designed to consider various contingencies and unexpected events, which tend to occur more often the longer you hold your interest.

Since you must prepare for contingencies, what can you expect?

First, there are always changes in the real estate market, such as rising or falling property values or the availability of tenants. Second, you can expect frequent fluctuations in the availability of financing. You may, for example, sometimes choose to refinance to reduce carrying costs or regain capital for other uses. Third, local restrictions on uses of your real estate can change, such as height restrictions, limits on new development, or rent control. Finally, personal matters can change for you and your co-investors (and lenders), such as a death in the family, divorce, or financial crises (including bankruptcy).

Personal Ownership. The simplest form for investing is direct personal ownership in your own name (for you and/or your spouse). This arrangement, however, does not provide any liability protection in case something goes wrong with your real estate, nor does it provide asset protection for the real estate investment or for your other assets. Additionally, all tax attributes for your investment appear on your personal tax return.

Ernesto owned five apartment buildings in San Diego; they were all in his name. There was a fire in one of his apartment buildings, and two tenants died. Ernesto was sued by their families and had to file bankruptcy. He lost everything.

You may also invest personally through a pension account or IRA. Generally, this is best when only ordinary income is generated from your investment (e.g., payments on a mortgage).

It is possible to organize even complicated interests in real estate in retirement accounts, including in Employee Stock Ownership Plans (ESOP). However, with the possible exception of an ESOP, there are very strong no-conflict-of-interest rules that will prevent you from being a "partner" in the real estate venture with your pension account. Additionally, in most cases retirement accounts that "share" in loans (financing) on the property as an equity owner will lose their tax-favored position. To work best, such arrangements must be drawn up very carefully with the help of well qualified professionals.

If you wish to provide for greater personal contingencies, you may use a trust to hold your real estate interest, which can provide a greater degree of privacy and some opportunities for allocating income to trust beneficiaries. Keep in mind that formal liability limitation is not available through a trust alone.

The available choices for trust provisions are unlimited. You must be careful to be sure the trust will meet your personal needs even beyond the particular real estate investment in order to justify the time and expense of properly creating the trust.

Partnerships. Partnerships are particularly useful when there is more than one investor. There are numerous types, including general, limited, family, and special purpose. This form of entity was preferred until recently, since in many cases few formalities are required and tax attributes can be allocated easily between partners.

Several years ago I bought an apartment building in the San Fernando Valley north of Los Angeles, with an old friend. I asked him to consult an attorney to draft a written agreement. His response was, "We're friends. We don't need a written agreement." I told him that to stay friends we needed an agreement in writing.

Then early one morning in 1994, a 6.7 earthquake occurred in Northridge. Our building was severely damaged, and suddenly my friend wanted his money back. But as I had insisted, we had a clear and specific agreement drafted by our lawyers. I asked him to read it and show it to his lawyer. A few days later he came to me to apologize—and we are still friends.

Again, however, partnerships only reduce *some* liability. The very simplicity of partnerships has frequently been their downfall. Since the formal steps required to undertake a partnership are minimal, considerations for unexpected future events are typically not sufficiently undertaken and documented. This lack of preparation can lead to disputes that could occur with a change in circumstances, such as when a partner divorces or dies, which can significantly alter a partnership's tax position and control over real estate interests.

Partnerships have currently been superseded by LLCs as the preferred business entity for real estate investing.

LLCs. In the United States today, the most popular form for holding real estate is the LLC, or "Limited Liability Company," because this entity allows all the tax planning flexibility of the partnership while also providing liability protection akin to what can be provided through a corporation.

(In some cases in the past, especially where business properties were involved, interest in real estate was held in an S corporation. This form of entity allowed most tax attributes to pass through to corporate shareholders, while also limiting liability for the operation of the real estate.)

There are costs to establish an LLC, including filing fees and for the professional help you'll need to document your intent regarding the investment property. There are also annual fees owed to the state where the LLC is organized and does business. In some cases these fees can be substantial (e.g., in Texas where annual fees are based on gross receipts).

Frank, a California real estate investor, bought a large apartment building in Dallas. He did not consult with a real estate or tax attorney. He took title under an LLC. A few months later, Frank was shocked to receive a huge property tax bill. When he inquired about it, he discovered that in Texas an LLC is taxed at a rate of 5 percent on its gross receipts. Had he consulted with an attorney, he would have saved a lot of money.

Generally, most experienced investors prefer a separate LLC for each real estate investment. A separate entity for each property allows for careful timing of the LLC operations to meet your needs and those of your fellow investors when the LLC is established. Additionally, the tax allocations and elections that are allowable each year should be reviewed annually with your tax professional to be sure your personal situation and the LLC documents are fully reflective of the needs of all the investors.

Although the LLC is the most popular vehicle to hold real estate for investment purposes, it is not always the best way to hold title. For example, if a nonresident alien holds title this way he may personally be subject to filing a U.S. return if he is an LLC member. In addition, if a nonresident holds title to U.S. situs property in his/her name and then dies while holding the property, the estate may be required to file a U.S. estate tax return if the gross estate exceeds $60,000. That is why it's extremely important to have the advice of a good tax attorney, who can help you make the right decision about what type of vehicle in which to hold title.

Local Taxes, Fees, and Assessments

Again, you can't move real estate. It's there; it *will* be taxed. Real estate is taxed at local, state, and national levels, because it's a convenient and readily available source of funds for government.

Your job, or that of your advisors, is to be careful about what tax effects apply as you buy, hold, or sell a property. The first taxes you'll face when acquiring an interest in a property are those from *local* jurisdictions.

Local Taxes and Fees When You Buy. Local tax costs include transfer fees, which frequently are based on a percentage of the gross acquisition price of a property. In addition, there are filing fees, title insurance fees, and your costs for financing, which will include fees for filing documents against the property to protect the lender.

If you're acquiring an interest in a Planned Unit Development (PUD) or condominium/coop, there will also be fees for filings with the homeowners association (or equivalent). You may also run into fees for assessments for various local utility and service districts that can be triggered by a change in ownership. You can frequently negotiate with the sellers to have them pay for all or part of these assessments.

In many jurisdictions (such as in California, where Prop 13 laws allow for lower assessments on property long held by an owner), the prior real estate taxes and other local assessment district costs are based on a percentage of the total assessment of the property. If the assessment was artificially low for the prior owner, your new taxes will rise sharply compared to the prior year's charges. In some cases you may qualify for a continuation of the prior low assessment (e.g., because you are a family member or because of local "tax holidays" to encourage new investment) if you apply in a timely manner.

It is important to review the prior owner's books and tax bills, but keep in mind that your new acquisition could well trigger a substantial change in the tax assessment.

Local Taxes While You're Holding. State and local governments tax real estate with the idea that you will use local services, including schools, the fire department, and the police department. As an investor, you may not be terribly concerned about those things, but you will be concerned about taxation in general, because it does affect the value of property.

Additionally, if you own property in a state other than where you live, you may be taxed twice on the same property. You may pay the local taxes where the real estate is located, and you may also pay taxes on your net income in the state in which you reside.

In other words, when you buy property you must be aware of the taxes you will pay while holding it. Find out what kind of assessment district the property is in and learn about what other tax effects are likely to occur. Keep in mind that governments also sometimes draw up new assessment districts. Additionally, commercial properties often have special assessment districts, and those additional taxes can affect your available cash flow.

In down markets you may be able to seek a lowered assessment for your property. If you acquire commercial property and have lost your tenants or are refurbishing your property, you may be able to apply for a substantially reduced tax (and assessment) until you find new tenants.

Local Taxes When You Sell. The same sorts of local fees and taxes will apply when you sell (or transfer) your interest in real estate that you faced when you acquired your interest in the property. These are local fees, and you can generally negotiate with your new buyers regarding who will bear these costs.

State and Federal Income Taxes

State and Federal Taxes When You Buy. Before you buy you have several options for how to structure your purchase in order to maximize the available write-offs (tax deductions) and other favorable tax advantages (tax credits) on your income from your investments (as well as your other income). These options should be part of your arsenal as you negotiate your real estate investment purchase.

For example, a first-time homebuyer with an income in the proper range buying a personal residence sometime in 2009 or 2010 qualified for an $8,000 federal tax credit. That credit has helped many people, but it was not intended for the typical real estate investor.

For you as a real estate investor the options of greater concern are tax credits (up to 30 percent of gross costs) for qualifying "green" improvements to the property (once you hold title) and the allocation of your purchase price to various parts of the property allowing for faster depreciation. Normal real estate depreciation for residential property occurs over 27.5 years; for non-residential it is 39 years. To take advantage of this faster depreciation, a study must be done to allocate the purchase price to those elements that will be depreciated more rapidly. Some items may even qualify to be written off in full in the first year.

The costs for such a study can be several thousand dollars. It's also important to be aware that your allocation to faster depreciated elements may increase the sellers' capital gain, which may be taxed at higher rates.

Moreover, if your fellow investors have different tax situations, such as higher or lower taxable income, or even if there is an investor who is tax-exempt, you may have the option of allocating tax attributes (including depreciation and tax credits) among investors in order to take the best advantage of available savings.

These options require your prior knowledge, and you must know the right questions to ask before you buy. The laws are complicated enough that you really need a qualified tax professional to help you map out your strategy and help to prepare you for your purchase negotiations.

State and Federal Taxes While You're Holding. If you did your planning before you bought in and have already begun working with real estate and tax professionals on a particular property investment, you still need to keep alert. Always keep extra capital available to meet unexpected events; they will occur.

Each year tax laws can change, and local taxes frequently rise. Be prepared by regularly touching base with your tax professional. Furthermore, financial circumstances may change—for you and your co-investors—making it important to consider new tax allocations that could be substantially different from those for which you originally planned.

If you're fortunate and have planned well, your property interests may increase in value, which may open up opportunities for refinancing existing loans. An increase in value on an existing property could be your chance to pull money out of that investment in order to increase your capital for other opportunities. What is particularly nice about refinancing is that it is generally "tax-free." The funds you may receive in a refinance will not normally be taxed to you until you dispose of all or part of your interest in the property.

Because of recent financial crises, new tax credits were created, including opportunities for faster write-offs for certain property improvements, which could be a valuable use of your capital. Such steps might even increase property values and rents.

Tax Segregation

As we discussed above, you can depreciate some assets on your real property investments more quickly than the typical 27.5 or 39 year terms. If you haven't yet undertaken a study for cost segregation on your investment property, you should think about revisiting the opportunity.

What cost segregation does is allow you to separately depreciate the personal property found on your real property over a period of five, seven, or fifteen years.

Tangible personal property in real estate is also known as "Section 1245" property. It includes items such as air conditioners; cabinetry; carpet; countertops; drapes; dishwashers; the disposal system; electrical systems, including panels and wiring; lighting; plumbing, including process piping; sinks; stoves; and more.

Tip from the Coach:

One of the incredible benefits of our tax system is that you can depreciate an appreciating asset (your real estate).

By depreciating the personal property much faster than we can the real property, we shelter the cash flow and save tax dollars now, meaning there will be more money available to pay down debt, to buy another piece of real estate, or to put in our pockets.

Please note that land is never depreciated.

The Cost Segregation Study. In order to take advantage of the benefits of cost segregation, you must complete a study. The process is well defined by the IRS, which issued a 154-page guide for their auditors to show what a cost segregation study should include. One requirement is that a qualified individual must prepare the study. There is no certification process, but there are requirements for experience, typically involving somebody with engineering, tax, and appraisal expertise.

A cost segregation study is normally performed by engineers who cooperate with those who have tax expertise. They must be able to understand how to identify from blueprints what type of property can be segregated. An engineer will actually calculate items such as the amount of the electric load servicing tangible personal property and compare it to the capacity, or the total load, of the building. Then they take the entire cost of the electrical distribution system and allocate it pro rata between real property and tangible personal property. These experts must also understand why a light fixture in one room is 1245 property, while the light fixture in another room, because it is the *only* light source, is real property.

What Personal Property Qualifies for Cost Segregation? For federal tax purposes, a court case involving Whiteco Industries defined personal property as having to do with maneuverability. However, the ability to move property without damaging it, although it is the foundation for cost segregation, is not an absolute requirement. You can have property that is very difficult to move, but also qualifies. For example, the kitchen cabinets and sink are difficult to move, but they do qualify for cost segregation.

Determining When to Do Cost Segregation. Typically, cost segregation is done on buildings with a depreciable basis of $750,000 and up in order to justify the cost of doing the study.

Additionally, in order to determine when to do a study, my company, Dynamics Capital, decides on cost segregation based purely on the net present value of the tax benefits derived during the earlier periods of property ownership against holding it long-term and depreciating it over the full amount of time allowed. You should consult your tax professional in order to determine these figures.

A cost segregation study is one of the few areas in taxation in which you can choose when you want to do it. The IRS has not come out with any guidance, and there has been no litigation regarding the timing. You can wait until it makes sense financially to do the study, especially if you have passive income losses. In order for cost segregation to make sense, you must do it when you have passive income (cash flow) to offset.

You also should know how long to hold the property for the cost segregation study to make sense. For personal property, you must figure in the depreciation recapture that will occur when you sell the property. Analysis of the ordinary tax rate versus the 25 percent recapture tax on the depreciated portion of the property shows that if you hold a property a minimum of two to three years, that is typically the break-even point for cost segregation.

If you don't plan to hold the real estate that long, don't bother with doing a study. But if you're planning to hold onto the property five years or longer, then it's very simple to do a cost benefit analysis to determine if there are benefits to cost segregation.

Furthermore, I won't do a cost segregation study on any property that is not producing cash flow. When I start having to pay taxes on the cash flow from a property, no matter how much, that's when it makes sense to do cost segregation. Another consideration is that if you're paying more in taxes than the cost of the study, that's also when it makes sense.

In 2006, some investors and I bought a 242-unit apartment building in Plano, Texas, just north of Dallas. When we bought it, it was not producing cash flow. It didn't make sense to do cost segregation. However, in 2008 the building showed nice cash flow, so we did the cost segregation, expecting to defer $800,000 in taxes. In the meantime, we used the cash "tax free."

Backdating Cost Segregation. You can go back and correct depreciation on any property by doing a cost segregation study back to

1987. You wouldn't go beyond 1987, because those buildings were under the old tax regime and are all fully depreciated by now, so there is no benefit.

If you buy a property, you can do the cost segregation at the time you buy it or a few years later. Let's say that you have owned a property for five years, however, and until now you have been depreciating it over thirty-nine years. You can do a cost segregation study now, calculate what you could have taken in depreciation over the last five years, and expense the difference presently without amending any tax returns.

If you have already sold the property or converted it to another purpose, you are no longer eligible for the cost segregation.

You can also do cost segregation when doing a 1031 exchange (read about 1031 exchanges below), but that requires an experienced tax professional—even many CPAs don't understand the nuances.

Tax Planning for Unusual Circumstances

If you form a partnership for your investment vehicle (this includes LLCs) and one of the partners or the spouse of one of the partners dies, or if an interest in your venture would otherwise pass to a new person who would have a different tax basis for their interest in the venture, your organizational documents may allow the accounts for that new person's interest to pass through on the books in order to allow new depreciation for property that has been improved. This is a complicated process, requiring the help of an experienced tax professional, but in the right circumstances it can be an exceptionally valuable planning tool.

Passive Activity Loss

If you have bought well, you may still generate tax losses from depreciation and other non-cash write-offs from your real estate investment, which may shelter your cash flow from the property and even exceed the real return from your investment. These "excess losses" are classified as "passive activity losses" (unless you are a "dealer" in real estate), which you may use to offset otherwise taxable income.

Passive losses can shelter passive income from capital gains, but many people who invest in real estate do not have legally defined *passive* income, so passive loss deductions don't do them any good.

But as long as you have an "active" passive loss (it's an oxymoron, but that's exactly what it's called) you can deduct the first $25,000 in capital gains. That holds true only as long as it's an "active" passive activity, which means you manage the investment yourself. However, if your adjusted gross income from other sources is too high, the $25,000 deduction is phased out.

This is a situation in which you'll absolutely need to consult your tax professional.

Taxes When You Dispose of Your Interest in a Real Estate Investment

Let's say you have done well. Your real estate investment has done what you hoped, you're about to sell, and you know you'll realize a significant gain.

In fact, the taxes investors are most often concerned about are those that occur when they sell a property, which is when investors make the bulk of their investment income. Therefore, in order to make the most of your profit, you must be aware that in some cases it will be taxed as ordinary income.

For example, many residents of California who invest in real estate don't realize that there are no capital gains discounts when declaring income on their state income tax return. The profit from the sale of the property is taxable as ordinary income, which may mean a substantial tax bill. California state income rates can be as high as 9.6 percent, and that is in addition to federal taxes.

Additionally, there is also a provision in the California tax code allowing the state government to take 3 percent of the gross price of the property from non-residents or for Californians if the property is not their personal residence. That's not a good deal if you don't make more than a 3 percent profit when you sell.

In other words, if you've made a large profit on a real estate investment, those of you who live in states with state income taxes will get hit with both state and federal taxes.

You must also consider local taxes for counties, cities, and towns. In Los Angeles, for example, the city taxes you 4.5 per thousand of what you paid for a piece of property as well as requiring a fee to record it.

When you dispose of your interest in the venture, you may face income taxes in the jurisdiction where your property is located, and you may also face an IRS tax bill. Your income will be measured by the amount you receive for your interest above your tax basis in the venture.

Taxable income may include far more than the cash you receive, if you have taken substantial depreciation and/or if you have pulled money out by refinancing. You are also treated as though receiving your share of debt on the property. In some circumstances in which you have received tax credits for investments in the property, you may also have to refund these credits to the government.

Fortunately, you have kept in close touch with your tax professional, who will calculate for you the amount of your taxable gain and otherwise take care of the complicated analysis of your tax position and explain it to you.

Additionally, there are a number of options for how and when to recognize your gain, or even to avoid recognizing it altogether.

First, unless you have been very active (generally making four or more sales annually) you will be considered an "investor" rather than a "dealer." As an investor you are entitled to lower federal capital gains rates on your gains (although not for state taxes in California, as noted above). The rate has been capped at 15 percent through 2010.

A man bought an entire hillside on which he planned to build a residence. He only used a small portion of that purchase for his home, but in order to get the city to allow him to build there, he had to agree not to build on the extra land. The city officials then said, "Why don't you donate that land to the city? We'll give you a charitable deduction for the value of the excess land." No one else was going to build on it, and he planned to leave it vacant anyway. He got a substantial charitable deduction for giving away that land.

A large capital gain may push you into the Alternate Minimum Tax (AMT), however. Your tax professional will advise you regarding whether or not you qualify for the AMT. In that case, recovered depreciation may be subject to a tax rate as high as 25 percent.

If you have had "special allocations" of tax attributes (generally, tax credits and depreciation), those may need to be reflected in your share of taxable gain. Again, that's where your tax professional will help.

Additionally, since this taxable income comes from an investment interest, you may be able to avoid a current taxation by either making a 1031 exchange (see below) or donating your interest to charity. Currently, you may give appreciated property to charity and receive a tax deduction (within your personal tax limits) for the full fair market value of the property. Caution: If you have a negative tax basis in the property you must recognize this amount as income.

In some very complicated cases, you may be able to escape current taxes by converting your real estate interests into a Real Estate Investment Trust (REIT) or similar investment security.

Assuming you have a large gain from your investment (Well done!) but do not want to do a 1031 exchange or give your interest to charity, you may defer recognition of your gain by doing an installment sale, which will allow you to recover your basis tax-free and recognize the excess as income over the term of the note.

In the right situation (an installment sale is not for everyone) the interest on the note could produce enough cash flow to live on, let's say in retirement. In such an installment sale, you pay taxes as you collect principal, pro rata. The more principal you collect, the more tax you pay.

> *There is nothing sinister in so arranging one's affairs as to keep taxes as low as possible . . . for nobody owes any public duty to pay more than the law demands.*
>
> *—Justice Learned Hand (circa 1934)*

Keep in mind, however, that Congress thought installment sales were too good to be true, so it passed a law putting a $5 million cap on seller-financed notes.

Additionally, when you sell with an installment note, you must protect your portion of the risk. What happens if the buyer defaults on the note? That's why you must collateralize the note with the property you sold. You can even cross-collateralize it with some other property owned by the buyer, so that you have even more peace of mind, especially if you sold to an individual rather than a big company. You can craft the note so that the buyer becomes personally liable for the debt upon default.

You should also take into account that if your property is in a state that collects state income tax, you will still have to continue to file those tax forms even if you move out of state. You can get around that problem in part by creating a corporation in the state where the property is located and signing over the note to the corporation.

Finally, as we stated in Chapter Ten, the best way to finance your real estate purchase is through seller financing. The truth is that it works both ways. If I sell a property and the buyer gives me a 20 to 30 percent down payment and then defaults six months later, I win all around. I get the property *and* I get to keep the 30 percent. It's not as worthwhile, however, if you take the note with a zero down payment. That's why I always require an appropriate down payment when I sell real estate with an installment note.

The Tax-Deferred (1031) Exchange

As we discussed above, when you sell a property, you'll pay taxes on the gain from that sale. One option you can use to minimize your tax liability when you sell real estate is to exchange one property for another. By doing what is known as a tax-deferred exchange, you can make a profit, reduce your debt, and still have the cash you need.

These exchanges are known as "1031 exchanges" (the number refers to a section of the Internal Revenue Code.) When you do a property exchange, you can sell your commercial property, take your profit, and reinvest it. A tax-deferred exchange rolls over the gain from one property to another as long as the investor buys a property of equal or greater value.

In other words, with a successful tax-deferred exchange, you can tear it down immediately. The standard is that the property be "held for investment." Raw land can also be used as an exchange. Neither are you obligated to keep the property for the same commercial use as it was used for prior to the purchase. You could, for example, exchange a commercial strip mall for raw land that you plan to build on and still gain the same tax advantage.

IRS Rules for 1031 Exchanges. When doing tax-deferred exchanges you must be careful. The process is not simple, and you must complete the transaction correctly and within the deadline. If you purchase a property and do not use it for investment purposes within the legal period of time, then you will lose the tax-deferred status of the exchange and therefore lose your tax advantage.

First, you must identify the property you want to exchange within 45 days of the sale of your property. Then you have exactly 180 days to do the tax-deferred exchange; that may seem like a long time, but time passes quickly. In other words, it's best to have your new purchase and your paperwork lined up *before* you close escrow on the first property.

When Should You Do the Exchange? When real estate has appreciated, it's often time to sell. If you plan to do a 1031 exchange, you will have to reinvest in real estate again. In other words, you should only consider a 1031 if you are prepared to put all the proceeds from your sale back into real estate.

When Will You Finally Be Taxed? If you hold a 1031 property for investment purposes and then convert it to residential, and you now have a profit, the profit will generally be measured from the time that you converted the property, and you will need to do an appraisal to ascertain its value.

However, you cannot avoid the tax; the property will still be taxed if there is a gain. In other words, if you do an exchange on one property and then sell the second property, you will owe tax on the gain from the second property.

What is "Boot"? Let's say you reinvest 80 percent from your first sale instead of 100 percent. That cash is not taxed at the incremental rate. It's called "boot," 100 percent of which is considered gain. It's almost like a penalty tax, because the IRS treats that 20 percent as if it was all gain without any proration between the cost of the property and sales price. That penalty means you will get the best tax deferment only if you roll the entire amount of the sale into the next property.

Three-Party Exchanges. Doing a 1031 exchange is not merely swapping properties with someone. When you don't want to do an across-the-board transaction, it's called a three-party exchange. In that case only one person completes the 1031 process; the other two people involved are just a buyer and a seller. You will "run" the 1031 and buy from one person and sell to the other. Moreover, you do not have to do the sales simultaneously.

What About Partnerships? The question I receive most frequently about 1031 exchanges is regarding partnerships in which each partner wants to take a property individually in exchange for a property owned together by the partnership. A partnership *can* complete a 1031 exchange as long as it is the partnership that receives the assets in exchange.

For example, if three partners want to do a 1031 exchange of a property owned in common and want to find three different properties instead, they must distribute the property into three tenants-in-common interests. Then each of the three partners completes a separate 1031 exchange, receiving the property he or she wants.

The Reverse Exchange. What if investors find a replacement property before they find a buyer for their current property? The 180-day rule then works in reverse. As long as escrow is closed on the sale of the current property within 180 days after buying the exchange property, it qualifies as a 1031 exchange. In that case, you can often use a bridge loan in order to complete the financing.

Again, as with all complicated and specialized legal matters, you should absolutely seek out an experienced real estate tax attorney or other tax professional for advice before ever taking on a tax-deferred exchange.

Tax Considerations for Non-Investment Real Estate

The $250,000/$500,000 Personal Residence Exclusion. If you own a personal residence in which you or your spouse actually live (in some cases this can be a second home) and you sell that residence, you are allowed to exclude up to $250,000 as an individual or $500,000 for a married couple from taxable gain.

Since 1997, however, you have not been able to roll any gain above the exclusion over into a new house. There is also a "two out of five year rule," meaning you must have lived in the property any twenty-four months out of last five years in order to realize this tax benefit.

In some localities (including a number of counties in California) certain older persons or family members may be able to keep a lower assessment for their real estate taxes on a new residence based on the assessment of the home they sold earlier.

Additionally, when you borrow against your personal residence (and a second home as well) you may be able to deduct the interest on $1 million in loans used to acquire (or improve) the property, plus an additional $100,000 on an equity line of credit against the property. Otherwise, most personal loans do not allow a deduction for interest paid. The points paid to acquire a personal residence are deductible concurrently, but those on a refinance may be written off over the loan term.

Keep in mind that interest and loan costs on investment real estate are fully deductible against income without even these limits.

Your Second Home: To Rent or Not to Rent. The $1 million limit for a mortgage that can be deducted from your taxes can be used either on your primary residence or on a combination of your first and second homes, i.e., your "vacation" home. A second home can be real property, a motor home, or a yacht. As long as it has a flushing toilet and a sink, it can be identified as a second home. You can also deduct the property taxes on both homes.

If you take that vacation home and rent it out for the summer or winter season, all your expenses become deductible, but if you end up with a net loss (because of all the interest, property taxes, maintenance, and insurance), and if those expenses exceed the rental income, you cannot deduct all of the net loss. In other words, you are sometimes better off not using a second home as a rental property, because deducting the property taxes and the interest as a second home may be of greater benefit than deducting the rental expenses.

Generally speaking, if you rent out your second home for less than fourteen days a year, you do not have to report any rental income, and you can still deduct your mortgage interest and real estate taxes. If you rent it out for more than fourteen days, you will need to report the income and can deduct the expenses.

There are some nuances in the law, however, so it is always important to consult your tax professional.

Other Personal Tax Considerations. As noted earlier there are now various tax credits available for first time homebuyers. Additionally, various rebates and tax credits are frequently offered for making your home more environmentally efficient (a.k.a. "green remodeling"). Similar tax incentives are also available for your investment properties, and some of these will help you increase the rents you receive from your tenants.

Other Tax Considerations

❖ Some sources of funds used for your investments, such as a Roth IRA, may be tax free. Others, such as an ESOP used to acquire "business property" may allow immediate tax exclusion and the opportunity to substitute into more liquid investments.

❖ Sometimes you may find an investor who has a favorable tax status (or who may even be exempt from tax) that allows you to leverage your investment returns by assigning primary use of the property to that partner. This is particularly true if the partner is a church, school, or Native American institution.

❖ If a tenant has special tax status, such as a non-profit or an insurance company, you may qualify for a real estate tax exemption.

❖ If your real estate use is favored in the locality because of its use (parks and recreation) or because of job creation ("brownfields" and industrial parks) you may also gain a tax holiday or even gain governmental subsidies for your development. Likewise, community clinics and low-cost housing ventures frequently obtain government inducements for their developers.

❖ Personal changes *always* happen, and they tend to happen at the most inopportune times for your investments. Therefore you should always limit your exposure to such problems for yourself and all your co-investors by obtaining a waiver from each of the spouses and partners of each named investor, agreeing that the venture only need deal with the respective interests through the named investor.

❖ You will also need language from each investor agreeing to indemnify the other investors and the venture from any and all costs that may be incurred by any claim or action by a person claiming an interest in the venture through one of the investors.

❖ This waiver will not insulate the venture from all potential problems, such as from divorce or other relationship rupture, from death, or from bankruptcy or other financial crises. Even if you're sure that this kind of issue will never arise through you,

you cannot be as sure about such disruptions from fellow investors.

❖ Tax laws change constantly. Keep aware and stay well advised.
  Try to keep your plans simple and flexible, and remain patient.

❖ There are always opportunities in real estate for the patient and
  savvy investor, which is why you should work with well-versed
  professionals. Keep sufficient capital available (especially by
  minimizing taxes) to be able to take advantage of those opportunities.

❖ When you have a gain, pay your taxes. There are legal tax benefits available, but be cautious about so-called "tax shelters." If it
  sounds too good to be true, it probably isn't legal.

There still are very attractive tax benefits for real estate investors.
Be sure to consult with your tax advisors regarding how to take full
advantage of them.

CHAPTER THIRTEEN

TAX LIENS AND DEEDS

*T*ax lien and tax deed sales are often a fast, easy, and effective way to make money in real estate.

Of course, tax sales are not new. Some of you might remember a famous scenario from *Gone With the Wind* in which the fictional Scarlett, now living in poverty after the end of the Civil War, schemes to marry her sister's fiancé for money—all because she doesn't want to lose the family farm, Tara, to a tax sale.

Tax sales will be a part of the real estate landscape as long as property owners continue to have to pay real estate taxes. Those property taxes are typically administered and collected by county and city governments. Homeowners and commercial property owners are meant to benefit from those taxes in the form of local government services, such as hospitals, parks, playgrounds, police, schools, and maintaining and building roads, bridges, and freeways.

> *Tip from the Coach:*
>
> *Tax lien and tax deed sales
> are the best kept secret
> in real estate investing.*

What happens when someone stops paying property taxes? In that case the city or county government has the right to replace that lost income by selling the property at an auction, also known as a tax sale.

There are two basic types of tax sales: tax lien sales and tax deed sales:

Tax Lien Sales. When the owners of a property have not paid their property taxes, the county or city puts a lien on the property and can then sell the lien to investors. In effect, the investor has become a lender to the property owner with the property acting as collateral.

The purchasers of a tax lien receive a certificate showing they are in possession of the lien on the property. In most cases, the buyer has the first lien position on the title—that's ahead of all other liens except state tax liens, including deeds of trust, mortgages, and other private liens.

With a tax lien sale, you're not buying the property itself, you're buying the tax debt. The amount of time an investor holds this "lender" status depends on the county or city government—it can sometimes be two or three years. When the waiting period has ended, if the owner still has not paid, then the investor can foreclose. Some counties then transfer the deed to the purchaser as a "No Warranty Deed," which should then be taken to a lawyer, who will register it properly.

Property tax liens can be a lucrative investment, because they are typically sold far below the property's market value. Plus, if the property owner is able and willing to pay off the delinquent taxes, the investor has the right to collect interest penalties, often at high rates (up to 24 percent).

That makes tax lien investing a win-win situation most of the time. If the delinquent taxes are paid off, investors recoup their initial investment, plus interest. If the taxes remain unpaid, the investors can foreclose and then own the property, usually for a fraction of its actual value.

Tax Deed Sales. When a county or state has already foreclosed on a property because the owner has not paid the taxes, it can then hold an auction and sell the property. That auction is known as a "tax deed sale." The buyer receives a tax deed to the property, similar to a trust deed.

The county or other government entity to which taxes are owed collects back taxes plus fees, interest charges, and court costs. The winning bidder becomes the new owner, obtaining all rights to the property free of all deeds of trust, mortgages, and liens.

With a tax deed sale you also have the option to contact the property owners, offer them compensation, and take over the mortgage, which is what I prefer to do. Interestingly, many owners don't think their property is worth anything. Some owners I have contacted didn't even know they owned the property.

I purchased a really nice building just outside San Antonio in a tax deed sale. The people didn't even know they owned the land! When I informed them, the owner's nephew paid the penalties and all the back taxes, because he didn't want to lose the property.

As in a tax lien sale, if you do your homework correctly you can buy full rights to a property for a fraction of the market price, again because property taxes are typically a small percentage of market value.

Many people ask me if they should invest in tax liens or in tax deeds. My answer? It depends on your investment goals.

If you're looking for a high return on your investment (I have earned as much as 300 percent), and if you don't want to do much work—invest in tax liens. In that case, you must have enough money to pay the taxes, sometimes as much as two or three years in back taxes and penalties. If you want to be more aggressive and actually own the property, invest in tax deeds.

State Laws

In the United States, the laws regarding tax sales vary from state to state. Some states are tax lien states, others are tax deed states, and still others have a hybrid form, combining elements of both. California and Texas are tax deed states; Arizona and Florida are tax lien states. Currently, there are twenty-seven states that offer tax deed certificates.

Buying tax sales is another area of real estate in which you must do your homework. Not only is each state different, but each county has its own rules and regulations. That means investors must *carefully* do their due diligence.

For example, the statute of limitations on the finality of a tax sale varies from state to state or county to county. In California, the tax sale becomes final for all purposes one year after it takes place. Even with respect to tax-exempt properties, that is the absolute statute of limitations for tax sales in California.

Buying tax sales in California effectively illustrates why investors must know the local laws. Once property taxes become delinquent in the state of California, there is a five-year waiting period before the property will actually be put up for sale, with some variation depending on circumstances.

Furthermore, when you buy a property through a tax deed sale in California, you become the owner. But if the previous owner is still in possession of the property, which is sometimes the case, it is handled just like a foreclosure. To take possession as the new owner, you must evict the previous owner through an unlawful detainer.

Additionally, you must learn the statutes in California in order to determine if the tax lien has priority or not. If the tax delinquency doesn't have priority, it is subject to the mortgage; if it does have priority, then the mortgage could be extinguished by virtue of the tax delinquency. Plus, there are all kinds of taxes in California that can create a lien on a property, including sales tax.

By contrast, in Texas the only lien ahead of delinquent property taxes is a state tax, not even federal taxes take precedence. Similar laws exist in Georgia, Arizona, and Florida. In those states, a tax lien or tax deed comes first, and the bank lien comes after.

Many times I purchased property in those states via a tax deed or tax lien, and the lender, as the secondary lienholder, paid me in order to redeem the property. At other times a second trust deed holder did the same thing. At still other times a partner, sibling, children, or someone else from the owner's family paid me to release the lien.

Although you would think lenders would be extremely careful to monitor delinquent taxes on properties on which they are the lienholder, lenders don't always do so. Either they are not alert, or they don't care, meaning they neglect to notice that the property came up as a tax sale and failed to redeem it rather than letting it go to the public for sale. As a result, many lenders have had to pay me a 25 percent penalty in order to redeem a property.

Colorado, as a tax lien state, has different laws. Let's say, for example, the value of the tax lien you're purchasing there is $5,000. Bidding starts at that amount and goes up. You also must bid on the interest rate you will be paid on the delinquent taxes, and the investors who win the tax sale have bid the lowest rate they are willing to accept against the tax lien.

In some states you're only buying a fraction of the property. If you have purchased 10 percent, then when you have to foreclose, you're foreclosing on 10 percent of the property.

Getting Started

At any given time, there are hundreds of thousands of tax sales available nationwide. That means that finding tax sales is not difficult, but competition *can* be fierce, depending on the market.

In fact, when the economy and the market are strong it may be hard to find tax sales that make sense. In a healthy market, I have gone to many tax sale auctions, whether on the Internet or in person, where I couldn't buy decent properties, because big institutions were buying billions of dollars in tax liens.

That hasn't always been true when the market has been soft, however. Additionally, there are more tax sales available when times are hard, because many more property owners neglect their homes and fail to pay their taxes.

The first step, if you're interested in knowing more about tax sales, is to study the laws of the state and county where you want to invest. The information is not difficult to find; most of what you'll need is available on the Internet. A list of profiles by state with details about tax lien or tax deed sales, such as the redemption period or interest rate, can be found at www.taxforeclosuresales.com.

The next step would be to contact county or city government offices for details about potential sales, individual properties, and local regulations—or to visit the county or city website. Investors can find information on most of the three-thousand-plus U.S. counties through the National Association of Counties at www.naco.org, by clicking on the "Find a County" link.

You can also visit specific "tax sale" websites, such as the free site www.bid4assets.com and an inexpensive subscription site, www.taxlists.com. Don't let the numbers of properties on the lists overwhelm you. Pick those you like best.

In addition to researching on the Internet, I like to call on people at the county or at a property in person. Because I'm very polite, I get the information I want, and it tends to be much more thorough.

There are also some good books on the subject; one of my favorites is *The 16% Solution: How to Get High Interest Rates in a Low-Interest World with Tax Lien Certificates* by Joel Moskowitz.

How do you actually buy a tax lien or tax deed? You should be able to find basic information through county and city websites, such as the type of tax sale, the time and place, and whether or not you can bid by phone, by e-mail, by letter, or in person. In the past, you had to physically be at the tax sale; you can now often do it by mail and on the Internet.

Here are a few tips to help you as you get started:

* Know exactly what you want: money or property—income or growth potential.

* Narrow down your choices from the available range of states. Focus on a particular county or even a particular neighborhood. I typically choose one, two, or three counties at most to work with, otherwise it becomes too much work.

* Consider the prevailing interest rates.

* Consider the local laws.

* Attend at least three tax sales in person before you buy. Why? It's the only way to learn how the process works. Make sure you understand which type of sale you are attending: a tax lien or tax deed sale.

* Before you start looking in earnest, put the money together first.

* Start building relationships with the people who work in the appropriate department of your chosen county or city government. These people are human beings who respond to human relationships, and they can often give you valuable, sound information about local tax sales.

The Advantages of Buying Tax Sales

Once you own a property through a tax deed sale, you can rent it or sell it. Of course, the major advantage of buying tax sales is that you typically buy a property for a fraction of what it's worth. I have never paid more than 22 percent of a property's value when buying via a tax sale. Many times I paid as little as 5, 6, or 7 percent.

That gives you an additional advantage, of course, in that you can turn around and sell the property for 10 to 20 percent under market value, which often means a quick sale, and still make a nice profit.

Keep in mind, however, that with tax deeds, you are buying at a higher percentage than with tax liens.

Another advantage is that what you spend to carry tax sale properties until you can sell them can be considered an investment expense for income tax purposes—if you're considered a "dealer."

Additionally, when you have a tax sale or foreclosure, it normally extinguishes any lease on the property, meaning that you can ask any tenants living at the property to vacate so that you can sell.

The Risks

Do Your Homework. You want to do your homework just as you would for any other investment property. You should always scout the area where the property is located. You don't want to get a property in a tax sale where you have to carry a gun in order to collect rent. If I wanted to do that, I would have stayed in Beirut! I *never* buy any property, even in a tax sale, unless I or one of my closest advisors first visit the property and know the area.

There is an exception to the "see it before you buy it" rule, which is if you have a lot of money to invest and you buy several hundred properties at once through tax sales. In that case, the law of averages kicks in and you will make a profit.

For example, if you buy fifty properties, and you lose $50,000 on three of them, but you make $15,000 on forty-seven of them, you're ahead in the game. But if you want to buy just a few properties, make sure you look at them before you buy.

Order a Title Report. As part of your due diligence it's important to research the title of a property in addition to finding out about any trust deeds, mortgage liens, tax liens, and judgments on the property. On tax sales, my company doesn't purchase title insurance, but we always run a title report. It's very important to have the title company provide the name of the owner and as much other information about the property as possible.

Notify All Parties. I have done tax liens in Arizona, California, Colorado, Nevada, and Texas. No matter what state you are in, when purchasing a tax sale you or the county must inform all the parties involved—anyone who has a legal interest in the property—including the lender, owner, part-owners, trustee, or contractor. Your job is to make sure they are notified. If you cannot notify them, you must advertise in a county paper twice, announcing the tax sale.

No Immediate Cash Flow. One of the risks of investing in tax lien sales is that there is no immediate cash flow from the property. In other words, you cannot look for tax sales to give you income to live on.

Governments Make Mistakes. The other main risk is that sometimes the county or city government makes a mistake. My company bought a property with a nice four-bedroom house. We visited the property, and there was no house there, it was just a piece of land! Some people at the county said someone moved the house, some said the house never existed.

In other cases, I've come across tax sales where the description indicated a house with four bedrooms, but in reality there were only two. I've seen a tax sale of a strip of land in Arizona along the freeway that was sixteen feet wide. We could not have built anything on a property that size.

In California, for the most part, once the tax sale takes place, it's final. The only real exception would be tax-exempt properties that have been essentially inadvertently sold; in that case the deed would be considered void.

My company bought eighteen acres of land in Georgia, but a church had already bought the land to build on. The county had made a mistake and did not transfer title to the church and then sold us the land via a tax sale. The church essentially said, "Wait a minute, nobody informed us about the tax deed." It took us about seven months to get the situation straightened out.

Taxpayer's Right of Redemption. When you buy a tax deed, you are the owner, but how ownership is transferred depends on each jurisdiction. In certain states, such as Texas and Georgia, even with the tax deed sale, you are not yet the property owner. In those cases, even after you have made the purchase, the owner has a redemption period in which to pay the back taxes and redeem the property.

If you buy a tax lien, depending on the state, you can wait as little as six months to as long as five years for the redemption period to end. If the redemption period is two years, and the property owner doesn't pay you, you can then foreclose or the county will give you a "No Warranty Deed" or a similar instrument.

This is another area where you must be careful. If you buy a tax lien and you don't pay the property tax when it is next due, someone else can then buy the property via a tax sale. In other words, you must have enough funds to carry the property until the end of the redemption period.

Record the Deed Promptly. In some states, the government does not record the deed after a tax sale. Additionally, you must make sure the tax lien or tax deed gets recorded immediately, because the taxpayer's redemption period starts from the day it is recorded.

Watch Out for Other Liabilities. In addition to other state and assessment taxes, there could be other liabilities to a tax sale property, such as toxic substances that you, as the new owner, will be responsible for cleaning up. That's why it pays to do your homework.

Noel bought an acre of industrial property in Florida for $27,000. He didn't do his homework and didn't know the state had a lien on the property that they would not release until a toxic substance was removed. The cost for cleanup was estimated at more than $3 million.

Noel thought he would ignore the problem, but the city did not. A few months later he received a notice requiring him to clean up the toxic substance. He ignored that as well. Then he received notice that the city was assessing a $50,000 penalty every month until he cleaned up the property.

Noel was devastated. He could not afford the cost of the cleanup, so he left the United States and went back to his home country of Switzerland.

No Immediate Tax Benefit. When you buy a tax deed, you're taking title of the property. It's just as if you bought a piece of real estate and closed on it in any other way. However, if you plan to sell it again quickly, you'll pay ordinary income tax on it. You have to hold that property for more than a year to get any type of special tax benefit.

However, dealer rules also apply to tax sale purchases. If it's your business to buy and sell homes, then you can deduct more losses, because you're a dealer. The more numerous your tax sale transactions, the more likely you will be seen, for income tax purposes, as a dealer.

Beware the Tax Sale Gurus. A lot of companies will sell you courses about tax sales for $5,000, $10,000, even $25,000. They will then also charge for research. You end up paying more than you'll ever make from tax sales. So be careful. Most of those people are after your money much more than they want to give you an education about tax sales.

CHAPTER FOURTEEN

YOUR KEY TO HIGHER RETURN: EFFECTIVE PROPERTY MANAGEMENT

*W*hen you've finally found and purchased the right property at the right price, go ahead and pat yourself on the back. But do it quickly, because you now have to focus your energy on managing that property successfully and profitably.

How to Get the Highest Return
on Your Real Estate Investment

Even a once-in-a-lifetime bargain property with all the potential in the world can quickly turn into a sour investment if you don't manage it properly. On the other hand, skillful management can convert some of the worst properties into gold mines.

Part of becoming an effective real estate investor means learning everything you can about property management. And without knowledgeable, effective property management you won't realize the highest return possible on your investment.

I purchased a 54,000-square-foot office building located on a busy corner in the San Fernando Valley in north Los Angeles—a great location. A bank occupied the entire first floor. Due to poor management the owner lost the building to the bank. Within eighteen months I was able to bring occupancy to 97 percent with qualified tenants and rent the space at 20 percent more per square foot.

A recent study by *The Property Management Journal* found that only 3 percent of landlords truly know how to effectively manage their properties. The other 97 percent manage by crisis, constantly reacting to problems rather than planning, acting, and taking control for maximum profitability. When handled properly, however, property management can be both rewarding and profitable.

Sure, management can sometimes be a headache, but the trick is to manage by planning, not by crisis. People don't get as excited about management techniques and procedures as they do about no-money-down deals, or terrific new creative financing techniques, but without effective management your project might fail, and you may lose your shirt.

The truth is that mismanaged properties are golden opportunities—if you're able to correct the mistakes made by the previous owners and managers. Typically, they haven't made huge mistakes; they've just overlooked details and have made small errors.

I bought an eighty-eight-unit apartment building in Colorado at a steal. The reason? The property owner chose to have the broker who sold him the building manage it rather than a professional property management company. The broker had no idea how to manage a property and didn't plan any management strategy. He was the "reactive" type who managed by crisis. He made improvements to the building or its operations only when he received a complaint. When the property owner finally got fed up with not seeing any return on his investment, he investigated and was shocked to find stacks of notices from the city that had not been responded to. When I came along, he was eager to get rid of what he saw as a problem property. He told me, "Name your price and take it."

Have a Clear Objective: Short-Term or Long-Term

To be an effective property manager, you first must know your investment objectives. How you manage a property depends on your intention: Will you keep the property short term or long term?

I bought a twenty-four-unit apartment building in the Mar Vista area of Los Angeles with the intention of fixing it up and selling it. All the improvements were up to code and professionally completed to the expectation of the buyers. In fact, they were one notch above other properties in the area. But we controlled the cost of improvements by putting linoleum in the kitchens and the bathrooms as well as installing plastic countertops.

We also bought a twenty-one-unit apartment building in West Los Angeles with the intention of keeping it for at least four years. Thus, we put tile in the kitchens and bathrooms. In buildings in upscale areas, such as Brentwood or Beverly Hills, we always add wood or marble flooring and granite countertops in the kitchen and bathrooms.

Short-term real estate investments are those you plan to hold from one to five years. Long-term investments are those you'll keep six years or longer. Which type of investment you choose will help you to make the right decisions when it comes to how you set rent prices and what types of improvements you'll make to the property.

With short-term investments, you need to be aggressive on rents, and not too concerned about having a couple of vacancies. You want to rent at the maximum amount the market will allow. Improvements don't have to be the most expensive or the most durable. They must only be adequate based on the neighborhood and the market. (But you shouldn't be *too* cheap. Use less expensive, though quality materials.)

With long-term investments, you want to be less aggressive on rents to keep the building full and cash flow steady. For example, if the market is at $1,300 for a one bedroom, you might consider renting it at $1,250 or $1,275. And I always charge existing tenants $25 to $50 less rent than new tenants. Additionally, improvements in long-term investments should be higher quality and longer-lasting, because you don't want to keep replacing everything.

Please Note: When the market is hot, you often don't have to do anything to a property. But when the market is soft or has stabilized, you need to be more creative and make improvements to meet the expectation of buyers, especially to improve curb appeal.

Remember: You only have one chance to make a good first impression. So pay special attention to the little things: stains on the walls or on carpets, chipped paint, caulking in the bathroom and kitchen, brown patches on the lawn, or dead flowers, an untidy or smelly resident manager's home or office, dirt (especially in corners or on shelves), green water in the pool, and so on.

Kevin bought a thirty-five-unit apartment building in the Beverly-wood area near Beverly Hills, California. The building was mismanaged and run down with a lot of deferred maintenance. He worked on fixing the inside of the building first. Although he spent a lot of money on advertisements, he was not able to attract good tenants. He asked me for advice.

When I visited the building, I found that the grounds were dirty, the grass brown, the paint chipped, and the fences broken.

I told him to immediately clean the grounds and improve the curb appeal of the building. Once he started cleaning up the outside, before he had even finished the improvements, Kevin was able to rent several units to qualified tenants. Potential tenants saw the difference and were willing to sign leases.

Also keep in mind that when managing properties, all the improvements and repairs that you make must meet the following three criteria:

1. Quality (no compromises).
2. Price (must be extremely competitive).
3. Timing (projects must be completed when promised).

Should You Manage Your Property or Hire a Professional?

Deciding whether to manage your recently purchased property

yourself or whether to hire a professional property manager can be one of the most important decisions you make.

Here are a few questions to ask yourself:

- ❖ How comfortable would I be managing a property on my own?
- ❖ Would I enjoy managing properties and dealing with tenants?
- ❖ Can I afford a professional property management company?
- ❖ How big is the property?
- ❖ Is the property close to where I live or work?
- ❖ How valuable is my time?

You must first determine the best use of your time. Where can you make the most contribution to the process? Is it mowing the grass, changing the faucets, painting the units/fences, or collecting the rents? You may initially need to perform all these duties, but it should not be for long, especially if you plan to purchase more than one property, or if you have a larger complex, or if the property is out of state, or at a distance from where you live or work. Your primary function should be to stay focused on your roles as entrepreneur and strategic manager.

Tina lived in a condo in Santa Monica, California. Then she bought a twelve-unit apartment building in Oxnard, an hour's drive north of her condo. She also purchased a twenty-unit property in Riverside, a ninety-minute drive east. After a few months of spending her weekends on the road, she came to me for advice. I asked her a few questions and helped her realize that she would rather live in Oxnard than in Santa Monica or Riverside. I advised her to sell the units in Riverside and the condo in Santa Monica. Now Tina owns seven apartment properties in Oxnard from which she makes a very good income. She's happy with the move and doesn't have to brave the traffic of the 101 or 10 freeways, unless she chooses to!

Your decision whether or not to get involved in the day-to-day operations of the property depends on the size of the apartment building you buy, your level of experience, and the level of experience of the resident manager you may hire, if any.

However, if this is your first purchase and the property has fewer than sixteen units, you will likely want to be directly involved in managing it. There is no substitute for the kind of experience you will gain while directing the daily affairs of your property. Of course, when you can afford it, you should hire a resident manager who can act as an assistant to you as well as manage the property.

Please Note: If there are sixteen units or more, the law requires that you hire an on-site manager.

Karim's Ten Tips for Effective Property Management

If your building is small enough for you to manage it on your own, you'll want to do it effectively and with planning. Here are ten tips that will help you be a better manager, so *you* won't be managing by crisis.

1. **Move-In and Move-Out Reports:** Without fail, before a tenant moves in or out you should have someone complete a move-in or move-out report.

I was once contacted by a lawyer representing a former tenant, who claimed he had been unfairly charged for damage to the apartment, namely stained carpet, a broken window, and a missing deadbolt. The lawyer claimed that his client had left the apartment in exactly the condition it was in when he moved in. However, because we had documented the move-in condition as well as the move-out condition with pictures and the tenant's signature, the lawyer quickly realized he did not have a leg to stand on. Case closed!

Even if you're leasing the property unfurnished, you'll want to agree up front with your new tenants regarding the condition of the unit. The same goes for when they move out so that you can determine how much you should deduct from the security deposit, if anything. I take pictures of everything that's been done in the apartment and everything that needs to be done. And when additional improvements or repairs are completed, I take more pictures.

2. **Frequent Inspections:** Inspect the inside of the apartment at least twice a year for leaks, needed repairs, and maintenance.

We inspected an apartment in a rent-controlled building in Santa Monica. When we got inside, we found a virtual zoo: at least twelve cats, fifteen birds, and some lizards too! Needless to say, the place smelled horrible. We reported the tenant to the city and were able to evict him. If we hadn't checked the apartment at six months, can you imagine the state it would have been in at the year mark?

3. **House Rules:** In addition to the lease, you should hand the tenants a well-prepared and detailed list of house rules, so they'll know exactly what is expected of them.

4. **Documentation:** Document everything you say and do with and for the tenants. Whenever possible, try to keep everything in writing: repair requests and dates of completion (including digital photos), notices, move-in and move-out reports, rent increases, late fees, etc.

In a ninety-three-unit building in Hollywood, we had a tenant with an "artistic temperament." He often fought loudly with his girlfriend and played his drum set in the early morning hours. We asked him several times to cease and desist, and we documented each request on paper: the other tenants' complaints, the police reports, and our notices to him. We also recorded all of our conversations with him. Unfortunately he did not acquiesce, and we had to evict. He fought the eviction, but we were able to get him out because we had proof of our long and well-documented struggle.

5. **Organization:** Organize your files; have a place for everything and everything in its place. Have a file for all important documents: records of city, state, and federal laws; offers; counter offers; purchase agreements; escrow instructions; due diligence; title insurance; fire and liability insurance; mortgage, etc.

   Each unit should have its own file containing all applicable repair records, leases, notices, etc., so that whenever you need something, it will be at your fingertips. The files could be electronic—with timely backup, of course—or hard copy, or both. Don't forget to keep files for past tenants for at least three years after they move out. I prefer to keep them for seven years.

6. **Insurance:** You may be tempted to minimize your expenses in order to maximize your investment return, so insurance may seem unnecessary or too expensive. But this is one area where you should *never* skimp. If your property is underinsured, and it is damaged or destroyed, your policy may not cover its full replacement value.

   Please note: It's a good idea to make sure you get an independent, professional consultation before you sign *any* insurance policy.

At the time that we bought a 144-unit apartment building in San Antonio, Texas, the market was soft and most tenants were living paycheck to paycheck. Several did not manage their finances properly and were behind on rent. The previous resident manager told me there were a high percentage of "skips" (tenants who break the lease and move out without notice). In response, I worked with tenants who had decent jobs, and made arrangements for them to pay rent twice a month, which better fit their needs and mine.

In another building in Arizona, we worked with tenants to collect the rents weekly. The tenants got paid each Friday and paid their rent each Saturday morning.

Because of our willingness to adapt our collections efforts in many buildings in different states, we were able to eliminate the skips.

7. **Collections**: Over the last few years, this is an area that has increasingly gained importance, as real estate—along with so many other businesses—has suffered from late and decreased collections. Threats of eviction, which in the past were the best tool for speedy collection, are no longer enough. A good manager must try to get to the bottom of individual tenant problem and treat them accordingly—just as *any* good businessperson would do for his or her customers.

8. **Keep Yourself Up to Date:** It's crucial to keep yourself up to date on what's happening in the neighborhood where your rental property is located. Check rent comparisons, amenities at nearby properties, and new jobs being created or lost in the area. Watch for new trends in the neighborhood and keep abreast of local political developments. Special attention should be paid to city, state, and federal laws that might affect your investment, regarding things like mold, harassment, or discrimination.

9. **Attract Younger Tenants:** If you want to attract younger tenants, equip the building with technological advances. Please note: Most of the long-term tenants in my buildings are either younger or older. In many areas, you have a choice of which type of tenants you want to attract.

10. **Smoke Detectors and Fire Alarms:** Without fail, have the smoke detectors in each unit and the fire alarms in the building checked twice a year.

The Resident Manager: A Make-or-Break Position for Your Investment

One of the main reasons property owners fail is that they don't treat their rental property like a business. When you're ready to hire a resident manager, or if you're required to hire one by law, he or she should be carefully selected and well-trained. And, of course, you should have a written resident manager agreement.

A resident manager can make or break your property, so make sure that you hire only competent employees and have an ongoing training program in place. (The same goes for hiring other professionals on your team: lawyers, CPAs, contractors, and subcontractors.)

A few years ago, I bought an eighty-unit apartment building in Phoenix from an out-of-state seller who lived in San Francisco. The rent roll showed sixteen vacancies, but when we inspected the building we discovered that there were only ten empty units. There were no leases, applications, or any written documents for those six additional tenants. We discovered that the resident manager, with no supervision, was pocketing about $6,000 a month! Who knows what else he was stealing?

Friends, this is not a rare incident, and it does not only happen in out-of-state investing. I have seen it again and again in every city where I own and manage properties.

Making the Move
to Professional Property Management

I have managed everything, from single family homes to apartment buildings, from shopping centers to industrial and office buildings, and from hotels to mixed-use properties.

After many years of doing this, I realized that I did not want to be involved in the day-to-day operations, the property management side of real estate. But of course, I want to set the policies, decide what needs to be done, and make the major decisions. That's why several years ago I hired a professional property management company to manage my apartment buildings.

Although many of you will become excellent hands-on managers, I recommend that as soon as you can afford it you hire a competent property management company. In fact, a competent property management company should be one of the pillars of your investment team.

Investigating the Property Management Company

Make sure that the property management company is experienced with properties of your size, category, age, and in the type of work you want done. Everyone sounds good on the phone or in a meeting, but only a few are really competent. Remember: There are no good or bad businesses, only good or bad management. You are putting a huge investment in their hands and, just like your resident manager, a management company can make or break your investment.

The following are a series of questions you should use as you are investigating the property management company you are considering:

Questions to ask potential property managers:

- ❖ How long have you been in business?
- ❖ Tell me about your property management philosophy and values.
- ❖ Tell me about your tenant retention policies and procedures.
- ❖ Would the on-site or resident manager be an employee of your company or employees of the building?
- ❖ How often and how thoroughly is financial reporting done?
- ❖ What do you love about your job? What don't you like about it?
- ❖ Who will be managing the property and communicating with me? The resident/on-site manager, the property supervisor, or the property manager?
- ❖ Do you manage properties similar to mine?
- ❖ What are your preventative policies and plans for property maintenance?
- ❖ Do you manage by crisis or by advance planning?
- ❖ Please give me three references. (Make sure you contact these references and ask the property owners about their experiences with your prospective property management company!)

Questions to ask the property management company's references:

- ❖ In what condition was your property when this company started managing it?
- ❖ How much money was spent to bring it to the current condition?
- ❖ Were the expenses within your budget? Were the improvements completed on time?
- ❖ Did they pay bills on time?

- ❖ Was there adequate and timely communication with the company? Were they available when you needed them?
- ❖ Were the monthly reports completed to your satisfaction?
- ❖ Did they aggressively market vacancies?
- ❖ How well did they screen tenants?
- ❖ Did you experience a high percentage of skips?
- ❖ Did they have an effective plan in place for tenant relations and retention?
- ❖ Are the property management company's values and integrity aligned with yours?
- ❖ What was their response to reasonable tenant requirements? (Don't forget that the tenants are your clients; they expect good service and relations.)
- ❖ How did they handle emergencies: earthquakes, floods, fires, break-ins, shootings, or deaths?

Questions for resident managers and property supervisors:

- ❖ How have you been treated by the property management company?
- ❖ What kind of training, if any, did you receive?
- ❖ Is training an ongoing process or a one-time event?
- ❖ How much authority do you possess?
- ❖ How often do you communicate with the home office?
- ❖ How often, if ever, do you communicate with the owners?

Questions for the leasing agents:

- ❖ Do you have a marketing plan?
- ❖ What are you doing to attract new tenants?
- ❖ How do you screen tenants? (Please note: This is the most important service a competent property management company has to offer you.)
- ❖ Is there a tenant relation and retention plan in place?

Questions for vendors:

- ❖ Does the property management company ask you for kick-backs?

❖ How promptly do they pay their bills?
❖ Is the company difficult to deal with?

Questions for tenants and neighbors:

❖ How responsive is the property management company to reasonable tenant requests?
❖ How quickly and professionally is the maintenance work performed?
❖ How are you treated by the property management company?
❖ How often do they communicate with you?

As you tour the property management company's other buildings, ask yourself:
❖ How is the curb appeal?
❖ Are the grounds, signs, landscaping, fences, and hallways inviting and in good taste?

Additionally, it's a good idea in your investigation to go to one of the company's other buildings and pose as a potential tenant. As you do, observe and ask yourself the following:

❖ Is the property management company aggressive or friendly?
❖ Do they seem to know what they're talking about?
❖ Do you feel like you would enjoy living there?
❖ How much is the rent?
❖ Are there hidden charges or expenses?

> *Tip from the Coach:*
>
> *Learn to manage by plan, not by crisis.*

Remember: The property management firm acts as your legal agent and has the right to conduct business on your behalf. They are generally given broad powers to make myriad decisions that directly affect the operation, and consequently the profitability, of your property investment.

Finally, don't try to save on legal costs; consult a lawyer before signing any agreements with a new property management company!

CHAPTER FIFTEEN

YOUR KEYS TO STEADIER CASH FLOW: AGGRESSIVE MARKETING AND TENANT RETENTION

Tip from the Coach:

In real estate we say, "Happiness is positive cash flow."

Fill Those Vacancies, and Fast!

D o you remember the two most important words in managing and investing in real estate? Cash flow! (See Chapter Six.) The reality is that empty, your apartments won't produce positive cash flow.

What high vacancy rates do produce are sleepless nights, gray hairs, and negative cash flow. Since I'm certain that you don't want to invest in real estate to look older and become poorer, you must put strategies into effect that will give you an advantage in terms of filling your vacancies.

As I've said before, you don't make big money from cash flow alone, but cash flow is absolutely necessary to help you carry a property in tough times so you can benefit from the growth in value when the market improves.

The vacancy rate in your building will have a major and immediate effect on your cash flow situation, and a consistently low vacancy rate will also have a positive impact on the value of the property.

A few years ago I bought a small office building near Century City in Los Angeles. A major tenant who had occupied 40 percent of the building had moved out. For three months the owner could not rent the space, so he sold me the building at a discount. I rehabbed the building and rented to seven professionals. Five of them also became my partners in owning the building.

Those of us who have been investing in real estate for a long time have experienced times of low vacancy rates and times where there are many vacancies that are difficult to fill. I sometimes have had to use creativity and incentives to attract tenants. At times we've even had to lower our standards a little, because the perfect tenants simply were not to be found.

In 1992, we owned a thirty-six-unit apartment building in Van Nuys, California. We tripled our advertising budget. We reduced the rent. We offered a $99 "Move-In Special," one month free rent, and no security deposit, but the vacancy rate was still more than 20 percent. We simply could not find tenants.

Additionally, as we discussed in the last chapter, when you take over a property there may be a need to fix the previous manager's mistakes. Evaluate the present tenant mix and get rid of undesirable tenants—or possibly even start from scratch. Either way, you probably will be faced early on with the responsibility of filling empty units.

When the market softens—and it always does—*every* landlord will have to cope with vacancies. You won't be the exception. Learning how to deal with vacancies effectively and efficiently will be a major factor in the level of success you attain as an income property investor or manager.

Remember: Any day an apartment is not rented, that income is lost forever. (You can't rent the apartment twice the next day!)

Karim's Strategies for Marketing Vacancies

Here are a few real-life ideas for how to rent vacancies fast. You don't have to do all of them at once, but you should do eight to ten of them *consistently*:

❖ By far, the best way to fill vacancies is to encourage tenants to tell their friends. Let them be your ambassadors and take flyers with their names on them to give to friends and business associates. Offer incentives to tenants when their referral leads to a filled vacancy.

❖ In today's computer age, you can't afford not to have a Web presence—a website for your property will work for you 24/7. It doesn't have to be too fancy, but it should display pictures of the inside and outside of the property as well as descriptions of the building and the neighborhood.

❖ To attract more sophisticated tenants, whenever possible equip the building with high-tech installations, such as a satellite dish for the whole building, special wiring for broadband ser-vices, or high-speed wireless Internet access that allows tenants to download movies and music, watch TV programs and videos, play games, and trade securities.

❖ If the size of the property justifies it, prepare a two- to four-page brochure describing the property's services and amenities as well as information about local businesses and their products or services, provided those businesses are willing to reciprocate by helping to market your property. This will help newcomers to the area *and* help you rent a few apartments.

❖ Place ads on websites that advertise apartments in your area, such as westsiderentals.com in Los Angeles, or on classified ad sites, such as craigslist.com.

- ❖ Place ads in the local paper as well as in free papers, such as the Penny Saver.
- ❖ Join tenant finders groups specializing in renting for a fee.
- ❖ Use the Multiple Listing Service (MLS), which means real estate agents will be helping to market your rentals.
- ❖ Advertise with major employers near the property.
- ❖ Post flyers in military housing offices.
- ❖ Post flyers in college and school housing offices.
- ❖ Post flyers in police stations and fire departments.
- ❖ Post flyers in hospitals.
- ❖ Place ads with church groups and non-profit organizations.
- ❖ Contact federal, state, and city housing agencies.
- ❖ Contact HUD.
- ❖ Contact your local chamber of commerce.
- ❖ Contact relocation assistance offices.
- ❖ Put signs on bulletin boards in restaurants, supermarkets, drug-stores, etc.
- ❖ Put signs on flags or poles.
- ❖ Put up yard signs.
- ❖ Advertise on billboards.
- ❖ Advertise in the Yellow Pages, both print and electronic.
- ❖ Advertise on radio, television, and cable.
- ❖ Market to tenants in apartment buildings in the area, with mass mailings offering special discounts of $100-$200.
- ❖ Make alliances with other property owners and managers.
- ❖ Hold open houses and parties.
- ❖ Talk to everyone you meet and know about your rental property.

Once someone visits or calls about the property, follow up with a picture postcard as well as by phone. If you leave a message, make sure it is clear, short, to the point, and most importantly, *courteous*. At our company, we only leave a message after the third try.

Remember: The screening process should start with advertising. Be clear and specific in your ad, but also be careful not to discriminate.

Make Your Units Rent-Ready

While you're working on advertising your rentals, you also need to prepare the units for showing.

Open the windows regularly to air the space, and burn incense to make the apartment smell fresh. When you're showing a unit, turn on enough lights so that it's easy for your prospective tenants to see everything.

Make sure the showers (and shower curtains) are clean (and hung properly). The tiles in the kitchen and bathroom should be freshly caulked. The unit should be freshly painted and the carpet either new or very clean with no stains or tears.

Blinds should be clean and functional. New switch plates and electrical outlet covers, preferably brass, are helpful. Appliances should be new or at least look new (our policy is to move older appliances from "A" buildings to "B" and "C" buildings).

The entrance and the inside of the apartment should be inviting and the kitchen and bathroom should appear attractive. The air conditioner and/or heating unit should function well (and quietly), and all smoke alarms should be up to code.

All of these things together will help you rent the apartment.

Remember: Any improvements or repairs that you authorize should be performed by professionals to just a bit *above* the expectations of the tenants. Don't overspend, but also don't be cheap.

I once led a seminar where I asked the audience, "How many of you have been bitten by a gnat, a little gnat? How many have been bitten by a mosquito? Stung by a wasp or a bee?"

Most of the people there raised a hand.

I said, "Wow! We have a lot of sweet people here tonight!"

The audience laughed.

Then I asked, "And how many of you have been bitten by an elephant?"

Of course, no one raised a hand.

"There are over forty of you here tonight, and nobody has been bitten by an elephant!" I said. "This confirms that it is not the big things that bug us. It is the little things that count."

Elephants don't bite, and the devil is in the details. So pay special attention to the details, the little things, and never show an apartment before it is completely ready.

Operations Manual and Job Descriptions

If you don't have an operations manual with a clear and specific job descriptions for each employee and task at your office and property, write one (or have one written for you) now. The biggest challenge most employees have is that they don't know exactly what is expected of them. The operations manual will help in the following ways:

1. Your employees will perform their jobs better because they'll know what to do and how to do it.
2. You'll improve communications between potential tenants and agents and thus help to rent more units.
3. The manual can be used as a training tool for new employees.
4. It will help you evaluate employee performance.

Additionally, an operations manual will show step-by-step how to market your vacancies, leading to a more unified, effective approach. Your operations manual should describe for your employees:

1. How to answer the phone.
2. What "script" or specific words to say to prospective tenants.
3. How to screen the tenant on the phone as well as during a tenant interview.
4. How to conduct a tenant interview.
5. What to do before, during, and after the tenant interview.
6. How to show the unit—what to say and on what items to put emphasis.
7. How to ensure that the tenant's application is complete (so that every line is filled out properly).
8. How to conduct a move-in/move-out report.

Your operations manual should contain written scripts in clear, easy-to-understand language for each interaction with tenants. All employees should practice these scripts again and again so that the words become second nature when speaking to potential tenants. Employees can use the scripts as guidelines and put them into their own words as long as the concepts remain the same.

The manual should be designed for all of employees, including the resident manager. Remember, the leasing agent is not the only one responsible for filling vacancies; it should be clear to all of your employees that marketing is the responsibility of every one of them, from the receptionist to the resident manager. Hence, they should all be familiar with the building, its amenities, its advantages and disadvantages, the area market, and the local competition.

For further training, use a digital or tape recorder and record all conversations with potential tenants—after asking for permission, of course. Leasing agents and managers should then listen to the recordings to find out their strengths as well as what areas need improvement. The recordings will also help you determine how the process can be improved overall.

Making these recordings will achieve two purposes:

1. Improved communication with potential tenants and agents
2. Better training for new recruits

Tenant Screening: How to Avoid the Tenants from Hell

One of the most important tasks of property management is screening your tenants thoroughly so that undesirable tenants don't find their way into your building. Of course, some people lie and do anything they can to hide the truth. They'll even enlist their friends and colleagues to give false information.

Whenever the economy is troubled, many people are living from paycheck to paycheck. Add to that an increased number of job losses and difficulty in finding the same quality of job and salary they had in the past. Plus, when there are a large number of foreclosures in the market a lot of people are displaced from their homes. All of those things put together cause people to move more frequently. Some of those people will try to falsify or hide their background and their bad credit. That means that you must screen tenants thoroughly and carefully. As you do, keep in mind that those who didn't pay their mortgages are used to not meeting their obligations and may not pay their rent.

Remember: As you screen tenants, be careful to ask the right questions, whether on the phone or in person. Asking the wrong questions can get you in trouble.

An elegant lady in her thirties came to rent one of our apartments in West Los Angeles accompanied by a seven-year-old girl. She told the manager she needed to move in by the weekend, because she didn't want her daughter to miss any school.

The resident manager, who was also a tenant in the building, liked the woman and didn't check her references or background thoroughly. The manager accepted the first and last month's rent in cash. That was all the woman ever paid.

It took us seven months to evict her. She was an expert not only at taking advantage of the law, but at abusing it. It also turned out that the "daughter" wasn't hers, but rather a child she had hired.

The Telephone Screen. Telephone screening is a must. I cannot stress enough the importance of screening potential tenants on the phone before setting an appointment to meet them. Doing so will save you a lot time and hustle.

Your tenant screening questions should be prepared in advance and in writing:

- Where are you living now, and why do you want to move?
- Where did you live before, and for how long?
- What is your credit like?
- What do you do for a living?
- How long have you been working there?
- Where did you work before that?
- What was your last income level, and what is your current income?
- How many adults and how many children will be living in the apartment?
- Do you have any pets?
- Have you ever been asked to leave an apartment or been evicted?

❖ When are you planning to move in?
❖ Do you know about the credit check application fee?

Patrick was one of my real estate students. Every time he had a vacancy, he put ads in the newspaper and on the Internet and showed the apartment to everyone who called. He spent several days, some-times even weeks, showing the same apartment with no result. He eventually followed my advice and screened tenants by phone based on the script above. He then began to rent each unit after about every third showing.

The In-Person Interview. If the tenant passes the phone screening, set up an interview with yourself, the leasing agent, or the resident manager at the property office. The final stage of qualification will unfold in your interview. But be careful with the questions you ask, and document everything.

A single woman with two children applied for an apartment. A credit check delivered a clean report. However, upon further investigation, we discovered that the social security number and address belonged to her cousin. Of course we did not accept her. She filed a discrimination report, claiming that we didn't accept her because she wasn't married. It seemed that the resident manager had asked her if she was married.

Because we document everything, when the city agency called we were able to give clear evidence that we did not discriminate against her based on her marital status, but because she gave us false information!

Many landlords find it difficult to ask probing, potentially embarrassing questions when they're sitting face-to-face with someone who wants to live in one of their apartments. You want to make potential tenants feel at ease, but you also want to know a little more about them.

Despite that difficulty, you must never forget that you have made a significant investment that you're trying to protect. Therefore, you want to rent to financially qualified tenants who will act responsibly toward the property and toward your other tenants. That means you cannot be afraid to ask the right questions.

If the applicant is accompanied by family members or children, ask them a few questions as well. You'd be surprised how much you can learn about a potential tenant from them.

A young paralegal applied for an apartment in Torrance and gave us the name of the lawyer she worked for. However, we smelled something fishy so we called to confirm her employment information. We were unable to reach anyone, so we left a message.

Unsatisfied with simply waiting around to hear back, we took matters into our own hands. We found the law firm's information online, but the number listed on the website was different than the one on the woman's application. We got in touch with the lawyer the woman claimed she worked for. As you might expect, he told us that he had never heard of her.

Two hours after our conversation with the lawyer, a man called our office, claiming to be the lawyer. His story matched the applicant's, but by then we were on to the scam. Of course, we did not rent to that prospective tenant.

If everything you've asked your prospective tenants passes inspection, you next want them to fill out the application while they're still with you. You'd be surprised at how much you can learn from their body language while they're completing the application.

All blanks should be filled in. Then make sure you see a Social Security card and a driver's license (including photo) and that the numbers match what's on the application. Also check the applicant's car and license plate number. What kind of car is it, and in what kind of condition? How clean and tidy is it?

If the applicant is not a U.S. resident, ask to see a green card, passport, employment statement, or whatever the tenant has. You want to see everything!

You also want to get a current and previous residential address. If you call a prospect's current landlord and ask what kind of tenant he or she has been, you might get a good reference just because the landlord desperately wants to get rid of a bad tenant. But if you can go back to the landlord of the property where the tenant lived before that, you'll get a much more open and honest answer—a more accurate report—on what the applicant is really like.

Personal references are generally family members or friends who will give nothing but good comments, so your best bet is to call an employer. But make sure you're reaching the correct person and not just a friend in disguise.

Other things to check for are:

* Is the true property owner listed on the rental application?
* Is the employment information accurate?
* Does the person really work where he says he works?
* Is the boss or supervisor's name listed with the correct phone number? (If the answer is yes, verify other employment information as well: date of hire, rate of pay, etc.)

A boyfriend and girlfriend applied for an apartment together in West Los Angeles. However, the name they listed on their application, as the property owner at their last apartment was not the true owner. We did some research and came up with the real property owner. Upon speaking with him, he confirmed that he was indeed the owner of the property listed on the young couple's application, but he had never rented to or heard of the two applicants!

Most people are honest, but there are always a few who will give you false information. Therefore, always be sure to double check the information a potential tenant gives you.

Please note: If a tenant lies on his or her application, in general it is *not* grounds for eviction.

We bought a twenty-three-unit apartment building in Santa Monica. Our property supervisor suggested we keep the current resident manager. Soon after we took over, the manager rented a vacant apartment to a well-dressed businessman who drove a new BMW. Three days after he moved in, we started to receive calls from tenants about the noise coming from his apartment every night between midnight and 5:00 A.M. We contacted the police and dis-covered that the new tenant was a big drug dealer!

We worked closely with the police to get rid of him. We also investigated how the tenant had slipped through our screening process and discovered that the manager had been trained to check only the current address and employer. The current landlord had given a good reference to get rid of his undesirable tenant! The "employer" was the tenant's friend. Of course, the fact that he was well dressed and drove a new car had helped to fool the manager.

Income. Finally, an important step in the qualification process is to ensure that your potential tenants have the income to pay the rent. Many landlords use a specific rule of thumb to qualify new tenants in terms of income. Our policy is that the monthly rent should be no more than 25 to 30 percent of the applicant's gross monthly income. We do not make exceptions.

Experience tells us that people who are stretched too thin financially are more likely to default.

How to Get Rid of the Tenants from Hell

Even with effective tenant screening, an occasional bad egg will slip through the cracks. It takes documentation to get rid of an undesirable tenant, once you have one. You must know your legal rights, obligations, and responsibilities. You must also have, in addition to the lease, a list of clearly written house rules. You want to make sure you enforce the terms of the lease *and* the house rules without exception. Then you should document every violation, complaint, and notice, as well as making transcripts of face-to-face or phone conversations. Don't forget to document the date and time!

Natalie was a single mom with two children from two previous husbands. She was the type of pessimistic person who if she found $5 she'd pick it up and complain that it wasn't $10. No matter what we said or did, she always found something negative to say. To her, the glass was always half empty. She was a nuisance not only to the resident manager, but also to the other tenants and workers.

In addition, she had frequent noisy fights with her boyfriend and children. Because we documented everything, including testimonial letters from other tenants, we were able to evict her. Here's the irony: Her previous landlord gave her a very good recommendation— obviously to get rid of her and her boyfriend.

DOs and DON'Ts of Property Management in a Soft Market

As I've said before, real estate is a cyclical market. When the market is down, you must be flexible enough to survive, but not so flexible that you take big risks that will eventually cost you more than you collect.

When vacancies are on the rise, finding qualified tenants becomes harder. You must take into account that you'll have to compete with other landlords. You also might have to lower your standards a little and soften your requirements, but be very careful not to cross a certain line—you don't want to end up with the tenants from hell, who have no respect for the other tenants, property, or grounds, and who don't have the ability or willingness to pay their rent.

Even in a soft market there are guidelines you should follow as you're managing your property. Here are a few Dos and Don'ts:

DO Lower Your Standards Regarding Tenants. If you don't, you'll end up with a lot of empty apartments on your hands. When faced with the choice between renting a unit to a tenant who doesn't meet *all* of your qualifications and leaving the unit empty, you should take the first option every time. In doing so, you're taking a calculated risk, not just *any* risk.

If you have a tenant in an apartment, even if you worry about the tenant's ability to pay the rent, at least you have a chance of getting some income. It's not the best situation, but it's still better than the alternative—a substantial reduction in cash flow.

DO Complete All Preliminaries before Your Tenant Moves In. Before allowing tenants to move themselves and any possessions into your apartment, be sure you have the following:

1. A completed application.
2. A signed rental agreement.
3. A security deposit and the first month's rent in the form of cash, a cashier's check, or a money order. If you take personal checks, make sure you cash them before you hand a tenant the keys.

DO Make Arrangements to Accept Credit Cards from Tenants. Whether or not you choose to accept credit cards depends on the size of your property, but it's relatively easy to get a merchant account that will enable you to accept and process credit card payments.

Additionally, since most tenants are eager to agree to your requests prior to moving in, have each of them put a credit card number on file with you, with the understanding that it can be used for late rent, property damage, etc. Doing so gives you an additional level of security.

DO Deposit Cash and Checks Quickly. Deposit all cash and checks in the appropriate bank account as soon as possible, and no later than the next working day. This is for your and your employees' safety. Plus, always give proper receipts for rents or other tenant payments and deposits.

DO Return Security Deposits Promptly. Give tenants back their security deposits on time, according to the law. At our company we return deposits within two weeks with all supporting documentation and a copy of all bills and deductions, if any.

DON'T Wait to Serve Eviction Notices in Cases of Non-

Payment. Don't wait around patiently for late rents. When rents are not paid promptly by the first day of each month, serve eviction notices on the third day of the month. You must do this regularly and promptly. Then follow through, or tenants won't take you seriously.

DON'T Make Exceptions. Unless you want to be a charitable organization, don't make exceptions to the rules or late payment dates. Once you do, you lose credibility with your tenants and managers, and they'll take advantage of you.

Once you break your own rules, there are no rules. Then everything becomes negotiable, "subject to" this or that. Soon you'll be spending all your time in arguments, negotiations, and outright fights. The moment you begin to feel sorry for tenants, think of your financial obligations to your lenders, your partners, and your family.

Remember: No matter how savvy you are, there are always people out there who are better at being a tenant than you are at being a landlord. In the rental property business, hard and fast rules and procedures are your only defense against financial anarchy and eventual bankruptcy.

Tenant Retention: How Keeping Your Tenants Happy Increases Income and Reduces Expenses

Tenant retention, should be at the forefront of your priorities. It is the most important task performed by the management company and your employees, especially if you're living in a soft market. Additionally, effective management will increase your income and reduce your expenses without sacrificing the quality of the service you provide.

Tenant retention reduces turnover, and thus increases the income and reduces expenses. Additionally, with every dollar you increase the rents or reduce expenses, you increase the value of your property by about $10.

However, for every 1 percent tenant's retention, the savings are the same as if you reduced the expenses by 5 percent.

In other words, keeping tenants is far cheaper than finding new ones. So, make sure you treat your tenants with respect, and respond promptly to their reasonable requests. In return, they will help you by taking care of the property and by telling their friends.

Jeanine raised her family in one of our buildings in Santa Monica in a three bedroom with a den. She was a very good tenant who was very happy with the building and the service we provided. When her two children went to college, she wanted to move into a two bedroom apartment, but none were available at the time, although one was due to become available within the next four months. We made an agreement with Jeanine that she would pay her normal rent for two months and then a discounted rent for the following two until the two-bedroom became available.

Our tenants are not only our customers, they are also our partners; we need to treat them accordingly, with respect and courtesy. We need to know as much as we can about them, their families, their businesses, their past lives and their plans for the future.

Although you want to have a cordial relationship with your tenants, remember they are not your friends; they are your customers.

Harry, a friendly Armenian, was a resident manager in one of our West Los Angeles apartment buildings. Both Harry and his wife became very close to one of the tenants and his wife, and began socializing with them. The tenant then had some financial difficulty and did not pay his rent for two months before we discovered it. We ended up working out a deal with the tenant to pay his past balance within a four-month period and moved Harry to another building as a leasing agent.

Remember: Only promise what you can deliver, either when leasing the apartment, or any time the tenant requests a service or a repair.

My company strives to attend to the tenants' requests immediately; whenever it is possible to fix a problem the same day, we do it. If not, we tell the tenants why we cannot do the repair that day. We also let them know when we'll be able to do it. Then we make sure it's done as promised.

If the tenants can't get your attention, a fast answer, or a fix for their problem—they're gone.

Remember: It is not enough to get tenants to sign a lease; they must continue to be satisfied with the building. Satisfied tenants will not only renew their leases, but will also provide the property, with the best and most effective advertising that exists: word of mouth!

Additionally, the building should have the desirable amenities, so the tenants feel comfortable, want to stay, and renew their leases.

When competition is fierce, you need to differentiate your property from the rest by not only providing more and better amenities, but also special services that make the tenants feel proud, to be part of your community.

We had an apartment building in the Westwood neighborhood of Los Angeles, and some tenants who had been living there for about fourteen months ordered new furniture for the living room. We volunteered to shampoo the carpet for free, but the vendor told them it would be nicer if they had a new carpet with a grayish color tone rather than beige, as well as fresh paint. The tenant then wanted us to replace the carpet and paint the unit. We very politely stated that the paint and carpet were only fourteen months old, and we could not change it. As a kind gesture we told them we would give them the paint and they could either paint it themselves or hire a company to do it at their own expense. We also allowed them to replace the carpet at their own expense. They agreed to those terms.

On many occasions, tenants try to have us replace the carpet after two or three years; for most tenants, this is due to neglect and a messy lifestyle. Here we have to be firm and respectful. On a few occasions we have agreed to share the cost, but in general the tenants have to pay for it if they would like the carpet replaced.

Our policy is to repaint the apartment every three years and replace the carpet every five years. The tenant has to move and put the furniture back. For a good tenant, sometimes we share the cost or agree to paint or replace the carpet earlier than our normal policy.

Another important concern tenants have, especially in uncertain times, is safety and security. Of course we can't perform the job of the police or sheriff, but we can work closely with law enforcement and take other precautions to help reduce the crime element in our buildings. In addition, all your employees should be well trained regarding how to handle emergencies—from earthquakes to fire and flood. In our buildings we conduct frequent drills to train the occupants as well.

Property management is not easy, but there are ways to make your job easier, if you understand a little about human psychology and are willing to work with the tenants, whether your tenants are business owners or residents.

Good communication is the key to tenant satisfaction. Remember that tenants have lots of options, and you and your team should do such a good job of making them happy that your tenants would be fools to think of moving somewhere else.

Tips for Keeping Tenants Happy

* Hire friendly employees.
* Set policies and procedures for employees.
* Train with goals of service excellence, and appropriate business philosophies.
* Evaluate and reinforce your training and philosophies.
* Compensate employees well.
* Praise a job well done right on the spot.
* Lead your employees by example.
* Operate your business in a tenant-friendly manner.
* Visit the property often.
* Communicate regularly with your tenants and employees.
* Give tenants a means of communicating, with the property management office.

CHAPTER SIXTEEN

TWELVE MISTAKES MOST REAL ESTATE INVESTORS MAKE AND HOW TO AVOID THEM

*T*hroughout this book, we've talked about most of the common mistakes made by real estate investors. They're important enough, however, that I have listed them here, so that you can refer to them easily and repeatedly.

Think about them. Learn them. Memorize them if need be, because avoiding these twelve mistakes can help keep you from losing your shirt, as I have done several times. That way you can learn from my mistakes without having to make them your own.

> *It's fine to celebrate success, but it is more important to heed the lessons of failure.*
>
> *—Bill Gates, founder of Microsoft*

MISTAKE NUMBER ONE:
LACK OF PREPARATION AND RESEARCH

You should never put your money into something without knowing what you're getting, where you're going, and what you want out of it. You first have to be clear on your objectives. Set goals and make plans for how to achieve them.

You must know what you're buying, why you're buying, and what you're going to do with it. Are you investing short-term, mid-term, or long-term? Too many people set out to flip a property without any idea of where they are going with it.

That's a get-rich-quick strategy. While fortunes are being made right now in real estate, the business of real estate investment is not a get-rich-quick scheme. It requires time, dedication, and effort.

Ninety percent of your time in this business will be spent locating and purchasing properties, researching, viewing, negotiating, and doing still more research.

Remember that most of your money is made when you buy the property. In other words, it's all about making informed, wise decisions when you purchase.

A word of caution, however: Don't take *too* long to analyze a deal. Good deals don't wait around for indecisive people. Many people take too long and miss an important opportunity.

MISTAKE NUMBER TWO:
EXPECTING TO ALWAYS WIN

When it comes to real estate investment, you're not always going to win. As is true with most businesses, it's those who weather the failures who will succeed in the end.

For example, when you calculate cash flow, appreciation, loan reduction, and tax benefits, having a negative cash flow is not always bad. In the short-term you can survive negative cash flow, but still have a substantial return on your investment long-term.

Whether you're looking at your first property or your tenth, you must stay committed until the end. You must keep your goals in mind and stick with your plan.

Don't quit at the first setback, but be disciplined and don't jump from one idea to another. Keep your goals written down and get support from other real estate professionals, mentors, and experienced friends.

MISTAKE NUMBER THREE:
THINKING REAL ESTATE INVESTMENTS
ARE ONLY FOR THE RICH

Real estate investments do not have to be limited to those with endless reserves of money. You can buy a property with little or no money of your own. There are many ways in which you can use other people's money (OPM) to buy a property: seller financing, banks, private investors, partners, etc.

Sometimes you may have to pay a higher interest rate, higher points, or higher monthly payments. But if the property investment is a good deal, those things don't matter, provided you figure out the dollars and cents before you get started.

Investing in real estate is a business. Make sure you treat it as a business, and your investment will pay in the long run, whether you start out with someone else's money or your own.

MISTAKE NUMBER FOUR:
HAVING NO EXIT STRATEGY

In any market, buying real estate solely for short-term appreciation is a gamble. But even in a soft market, if you buy real estate to hold for seven years or more, the chances are you will come out on top. You can buy a property, flip it in a year or less, and still do fine. But remember, that is *speculation*, not investment.

Prior to the subprime crisis, many people made a lot of money speculating, because they were at the right place at the right time. Many other investors also lost a fortune because of bad timing. Real estate speculation is like surfing; if you don't catch the wave at the right time, you'll wipe out.

Even with careful planning, external influences beyond your control will pop up from time to time. There will be times when, despite your thorough research, a property doesn't perform as well as you like, or you can't sell it at the price you want. That means you should never enter into a project in which you can't afford unanticipated holding costs. If you're prepared for these unforeseen circumstances with an appropriate exit strategy, you'll be fine.

The need to buy real estate and sell it again as quickly as possible is understandable. After all, every month you're making a substantial mortgage payment. But in investment terms, sometimes it's better to hang onto a property.

As an informed investor, you should already know what rate of return you need and when it's appropriate to sell a property in order to get that rate. In other words, don't sell a property too early. There's no shame in holding onto a good property if the market isn't agreeable at the time you're looking to sell.

Holding onto a property when necessary can mean additional cash flow, tax benefits, and equity growth. If you're a *smart investor* and buy a good deal at the right time—and keep it a little longer than planned, if necessary—appreciation on your investment property can be substantial.

MISTAKE NUMBER FIVE:
TRUSTING THE SELLERS' AND BROKERS' NUMBERS

Most sellers and brokers are biased. Somehow, intentionally or not, they leave out many of a property's expenses and overestimate its income. Take any appraisal the seller hands you in the spirit that it was intended, as a marketing piece. An appraisal isn't really meaningful unless you hire the appraiser and give the instructions yourself. I can influence an appraiser to value a $100,000 property for as little as $80,000 or as high as $120,000. That's a 20 percent variance, and it's a big difference in a marginal deal.

Don't get caught up in the excitement of a new deal. Verify any numbers given to you by the sellers or their agents. Claims of extremely high rates of return run rampant. The rents listed on the sellers' paperwork may or may not be accurate. Additionally, don't let the seller overestimate market rents. Do your own market survey.

Check everything: market rents, payment history, taxes, expenses, collections, future variables, etc. It also helps to know why the sellers are selling and how motivated they are.

MISTAKE NUMBER SIX:
INSUFFICIENT OR NEGATIVE CASH FLOW

It's okay to experience negative cash flow for a *short* period, provided you have enough reserves to carry the property longer, if necessary. However, property that needs cash every month can drain your working capital, leaving you no funds for other projects. Plus, who needs that kind of stress, frustration, and pain?

Furthermore, a strain on your cash flow may cause you to sell your investment before the benefits of ownership are ever realized. There's no point having a potential $100,000 profit up your sleeve if you can't pay your bills and lose the property. Unless you have sufficient cash reserves, I highly recommend that you find other sources of capital to fund your investment, including OPM.

Remember, the most two important words in real estate investing are CASH FLOW.

MISTAKE NUMBER SEVEN:
UNDERESTIMATING THE TIME IT TAKES TO FLIP, FIX, RENT, OR SELL

I have bought many properties from investors who get stuck with holding costs that are too much for them to handle. Completing repairs and construction and getting licenses and permits often can take much longer than originally estimated and can also cost much more than budgeted. As much as possible, it's important to correctly estimate the amount of time needed for improvements as well as cash flow, capital appreciation, tax benefits, and equity pay down, *before* you make the investment.

MISTAKE NUMBER EIGHT:
FAILURE TO DO A THOROUGH INSPECTION

When investing your hard earned money, be sure to use sound business judgment. That means always getting a professional inspection before you purchase any property. Hire a professional inspector, or if you're experienced you can do it yourself. Check everything from the roof to the foundation. Don't overlook anything; ask tenants about pest problems, structural damage, and recurring problems.

Additionally, you should inspect, approve, and confirm all relevant documents. The list of documents that need to be proofed can be overwhelming to the first-time investor: CCRs (covenants, conditions and restrictions), building permits, buy laws, health licenses, inspection reports, insurance, laundry leases, loan documents, mineral leases, purchase contracts, rental and lease applications, title policies, and zoning laws.

If you don't have the experience or the time, don't attempt to do these inspections alone. The right professional can remove most of the stress, save you money, and bring your transaction to a close.

MISTAKE NUMBER NINE:
LACK OF ADEQUATE INSURANCE

Investment property brings liability: tenants, cars, cleaning facilities, parking lots, property liability, and so on. The list is quite extensive. Adequate insurance coverage is an absolute must. Be sure to consult with a competent insurance professional to protect your hard-earned assets.

In 1997, Joe, one of my associates, left my company to start his own real estate syndication business. In four years, he syndicated six properties and was relatively successful. Then a tenant's boyfriend sued Joe; the boyfriend claimed he had slipped on wet stairs and hurt his neck and lower back. Unfortunately, Joe was vulnerable. He didn't have the proper insurance and had bought everything in his own name with no trust or legal entity to protect him. Needless to say, he was forced to file bankruptcy and lost everything.

MISTAKE NUMBER TEN:
MISMANAGEMENT

Hire competent resident managers for your rental properties. Check their references carefully and take the time to train them. Remember, your resident manager can make or break your investment.

Your resident manager should know how to select good, qualified tenants by screening them properly. Train your resident manager to properly check references from previous landlords and employers as well as financial references, credit, and judgments. A little work up front can avoid tremendous problems later.

MISTAKE NUMBER ELEVEN:
INEFFECTIVE MARKETING AND HIGH VACANCY RATES

Just placing bandit signs in neighborhoods and intersections without planning, testing, and reviewing the quality response rate is not an effective use of your time and money. Instead, identify marketing strategies that work and stick with them. Some approaches work better than others. Learn what works and what doesn't work in your area.

Not only will you market properties for sale, but you'll also need to market your rental vacancies and work on tenant retention. High turnover and lease terminations are your biggest rental property expense. Treat your tenants with respect and respond as quickly as possible to their needs, or train your resident manager to do so. It's a lot less costly in the long run to take care of little problems before they become big problems.

MISTAKE NUMBER TWELVE:
TRYING TO GO IT ALONE

To succeed in real estate investing, you must have a team of professionals in place and consult with them regularly. Make sure that you really listen to them. Members of your team should include an appraiser, attorney, contractor, CPA, insurance agent, leasing agent, mortgage broker/banker, property inspector, property manager, and real estate broker.

Don't be cheap. Consult the proper professionals before entering into any real estate transaction. Among other things, you should consult an investment advisor and have someone physically check the property so you'll know if a particular property is the right investment for you.

It's tangible, it's solid, it's beautiful.
It's artistic, from my standpoint,
and I just love real estate.

—Donald Trump, real estate developer

CHAPTER SEVENTEEN

FREQUENTLY ASKED QUESTIONS

*T*he following are the most frequently asked questions from my company's monthly real estate seminars. The answers are gleaned from the experience of our panel of experts, who between them have more than two hundred years of cumulative experience working in real estate.

"Why are real estate investors so edgy?"

Investors are edgy in the current economy for a variety of reasons:

* ❖ The recent subprime mortgage crisis created tremendous uncertainty, not only for the single family home and commercial real estate sectors, but also for the global economy.

* ❖ U.S. homes overall lost $2 trillion in value in 2008.

* ❖ Housing sales dropped substantially, housing inventory is increasing, and properties are taking longer to sell.

* ❖ There's a gap between seller and buyer expectations. We are seeing more listings expire, and buyers aren't chasing properties with the same intensity.

* ❖ The number of foreclosure properties have skyrocketed, putting more stress on housing prices.

* ❖ About 10 percent of the nation's homeowners fell behind on their loan payments or were in foreclosure during the third quarter of 2008.

* ❖ As of this writing, 11.7 million Americans are "underwater" on

their mortgages; they owe more to the lender than their homes are worth.

❖ Increasing unemployment rates are creating more tenant vacancies across all property types.

❖ During the previous real estate bubble, rents for both residential and commercial properties reached astronomical levels, and it was getting harder to collect the high rents. The market, however, is changing rapidly; both rents and real estate prices are dropping fast.

There is also *good* news in the current market. Since the Fed announced a plan to purchase $500 billion in mortgage-backed securities on November 25, 2008, interest rates on conforming fixed-rate mortgages dropped to levels unseen in a long time. That means money is cheap to borrow and that *smart investors* have a significant opportunity to make lucrative deals.

"I've been thinking about real estate investing for some time. But I think I missed the boat, and I'm afraid prices will continue to go down. When is a good time to invest?"

Real estate is a cyclical business. Sometimes it's easy to find good deals, and sometimes not. In any economic cycle, however, *smart investors* always have opportunities to make money in real estate.

For example, in an economic downturn you can often find good deals on fixer-uppers and foreclosures. Plus, what you add to a building's intrinsic value can be harnessed once the economy improves.

It's not about investing in a good or bad market. Rather, it's about finding the best real estate opportunities regardless of market condition.

"Where should I make my first investment?"

For the first-time real estate investor, we recommend buying a one-to-four unit residential property in a low- to middle-income neighborhood within a thirty-minute drive from where you live. You want something that's within your budget and doesn't require too much initial capital. Moreover, if the property is close to you, it's easier to inspect it, make repairs, and show it to potential tenants.

"How can I make money on a fixer-upper?"

The most profitable fixer-uppers need only cosmetic work, such as paint, landscaping, new light fixtures, or new carpeting. Avoid properties that need major repairs, such as a new roof, removal of walls, foundation repair, or structural work. Once you gain enough experience and are comfortable working with contractors, however, you can explore adding rooms, bathrooms, second stories, and other property features, as appropriate.

"How much should I spend on fixing up a property?"

Our rule of thumb: For every $1 you spend you should expect to increase the value of the property by at least $2 to $3. If that's not realistic, then you should spend your money (more wisely) elsewhere.

"Once I select the type of property I want and know the area where I want to buy, how do I find a good deal?"

Below are a few steps to help you find the best deal in a specific area:

* Drive through the neighborhood and look for distressed or neglected properties; these typically will have dry grass, chipped paint, or broken fences.
* Look in classified ads in local newspapers.
* Consult real estate agents.
* Look for notice of defaults and foreclosures.
* Check with government agencies.
* Search the Internet.

"I'm ambitious, but I don't have any money. I know how to repair houses, and I'm willing to learn and work hard. What's the best way for someone like me to start building wealth in real estate?"

The best way to start investing in real estate is to leverage the experience and money of other savvy investors by forming partnerships. In these situations, you can offer your expertise, time, and energy while the other investors offer the capital. If you don't have this type of access, my company, Dynamics Capital Group, may be able to help match you with an appropriate investor or group.

"What is a FICO score?"

FICO scoring, or credit-risk scoring, is based on a mathematical model developed by Fair, Isaac and Company (now known as Fair Isaac Corporation), which draws on consumer data kept within the nation's three largest credit bureaus: Experian, Equifax, and Trans Union. The higher the score, the more the person is considered to be creditworthy.

Here is a general breakdown of FICO scores:

❖ 700 and higher means excellent or very good credit.
❖ 680 to 699 means good credit, which should allow you to get a typical loan.
❖ 620 to 679 is good, but loan terms may not be very generous.
❖ 580 to 619 is still loan-worthy, but loan terms can be expensive for the borrower.
❖ 500 to 580 is considered poor credit and qualifying for a loan may be difficult.
❖ 499 and below typically requires borrowers to repair their credit before they will be able to qualify for a fair loan.

"Is now a good time to finance a deal, considering the current credit market?"

You might have a hard time financing a deal if you're looking for 100 percent financing. However, with a 20 to 30 percent down payment, depending on the type of property and the location, whether you have a good credit, and if the purchase price is right, you should be able to find financing. In addition, private money is a great alternative. There are many sources out there willing to fund your next deal.

"How can I raise investment money from private sources, and what are 'hard money' lenders?"

There are plenty of private sources that can be used to raise investment money. Close family and friends are usually the first ones to ask; however, be aware that some may not have the positive reaction you hoped for.

Another source is via hard money lenders, who are often the fastest way to get private money. Typically, they'll loan money based on the equity and the quality of the deal. If the deal is less significant, they might lend you less than you asked or charge you a higher interest rate.

Additionally, there are many other sources available, including large national lenders, local banks, conduit lenders, and angel investors.

A friend of mine used to work for a gentleman whom he took out for his ninety-sixth birthday. The man still board surfs and is an avid skier and does up to eighty speeches a year around the country at $25,000 a speech. That man's name is Art Linkletter. My friend said to him, "Art, when I worked for you in the sixties you gave me a motto that I've lived by ever since."

He asked, "What did I tell you?"

"You told me: 'Find something you like to do, and you'll never work another day in your life.' Do you still espouse that same motto?"

"No, I've changed it. My new one is this: What's important in life is not how many times you breathe, but how many times you're left breathless. I ski and surf and give speeches, so I make a lot of money, but if you don't have those kinds of passions, you'd better find some."

"How can I ensure that people trust me enough to give me investment money?"

First, you must be prepared and professional. Have a structured presentation, and don't come off as desperate. Remember to focus on the property more than on their trust in you. If you give potential investors a presentation that shows you've done the research and understand every aspect of the deal, you'll gain their trust and, in turn, their money. If they decide not to invest this time, remember that there are plenty of other willing resources.

Whatever happens, stay confident; your positive attitude could help persuade the next lender.

GLOSSARY

Some of the following terms are found throughout this book, some are not. All will be helpful to you as a *smart real estate investor*.

Abstract of Judgment: A summary of a money judgment obtained in court. When this summary or abstract is recorded in the county recorder's office, in some states the judgment becomes a lien on the debtor's property.

Abstract of Title: A summary prepared by a licensed abstractor of all documents recorded in the public records of the political subdivision where a piece of land is located. An abstract in some states or areas is reviewed by an attorney or other experienced title examiner to determine the status of title. Today, abstractors provide actual copies of the records rather than an abstract of each document.

Abatement: In real estate, abatement typically refers to a reduction in taxes or rent.

Acceleration Clause: Clause in a deed of trust or mortgage that accelerates or hastens the time when the indebtedness is due. Some deeds of trust contain an acceleration clause stating that the note shall become due immediately upon the sale of the property.

Acknowledgement: A formal declaration before a duly authorized officer, such as a notary public, by a person who has executed an instrument that such execution is his own act and deed. An acknowledgment is necessary when an instrument, such as a deed of trust, is recorded.

Adjustable Mortgage Loan (AML): Mortgage loans in which the interest rate is periodically adjusted to more closely coincide with current rates. The amounts and times of adjustment are agreed to at the inception of the loan. Also called: Adjustable Rate Loan, Adjustable Rate Mortgage (ARM), Flexible Rate Loan, or Variable Rate Loan.

Affidavit: A written statement or declaration sworn to before an officer who has authority to administer an oath.

Agent: One who has authorization, either expressed or implied, to act for or represent another party (usually representing the seller) or in business matters, such as issuing title insurance policies on behalf of a title insurer.

Agreement of Sale: A written contract entered into between the seller and buyer for sale of real property on an installment or deferred payment plan. Also called: Agreement to Convey, long form Security Agreement, or a Real Estate Installment Contract.

Amendment: A change that alters, adds to, or corrects part of an agreement without changing its principal idea or essence.

Amortized Loan: A loan that is paid off, both in interest and principal, by regular payments that are equal or nearly equal.

Annual Percentage Rate (APR): The yearly interest percentage of a loan as expressed by the actual rate of interest paid. For example, 6 percent add-on interest would be much more than 6 percent simple interest, even though both would say 6 percent. The APR is disclosed as a requirement of federal truth in lending statutes.

Appraisal: An estimate of the value of a property resulting from analysis of facts about the property; an opinion of a property's value.

Assumption: A loan assumption occurs when a buyer takes title to a property and assumes liability for paying an existing note secured by a deed of trust against the property.

Bankruptcy: A proceeding under federal, or in some instances state, laws by which the property of a debtor is protected by the court and may be divided among the debtor's creditors and the debtor.

Blanket or Trust Deed: A mortgage or trust deed that covers more than one lot or parcel of real property, often an entire subdivision. As individual lots are sold, a partial reconveyance from the blanket mortgage is obtained.

Breach of Contract: Failure of a party to perform the terms of a contract in whole or part without legal excuse.

Broker's Proforma: A document, usually prepared by the seller's broker, describing, among other things, the property, its location, amenities, income and expenses, and the asking price.

Building Contract: An agreement between an owner or lessee and a building contractor setting forth terms relating to the construction of a structure.

Buy-down: A payment to the lender from the seller, buyer, or third party causing the lender to reduce the interest rate during the early years of a loan. The buy-down usually takes place in the first five years of a loan.

Capitalization Rate (CAP Rate): The percentage (acceptable to an average buyer) used to determine the value of income property. Also the net operating income divided by a factor.

Certificate of Title: A written opinion, executed by the examining attorney, stating that title is vested as stated.

Close of Escrow, Closing: The date the documents are recorded and title passes from seller to buyer. On that date the buyer becomes the legal owner, and title insurance becomes effective.

Cloud on Title: An irregularity, possible claim, or encumbrance that could adversely affect or impair the title of a property.

Coinsurance: A transaction in which each of two or more insurers assumes a designated portion of the liability for the total risk; each is liable for a portion of the loss. (See also: Reinsurance.)

Collateral Security: Most commonly used to mean some security in addition to the personal obligation of the borrower.

Commitment: A binding contract with a title company to issue a specific title policy.

Community Property: Property acquired by husband, wife, or both during marriage that gives each spouse an interest in a property, whether or not each appears on the title.

Comparative Market Analysis (CMA): A comparison of similar recently sold properties in a given area in order to estimate the value of the property for sale.

Comparable Sales: Sales that have similar characteristics as the subject property, used for analysis in the appraisal. Commonly called "comps."

Condemnation: The taking of private property by the government for public use, as for a street or a storm drain, upon making just compensation to the owner. This right or power of government to take property for a necessary public use is called "eminent domain."

Constructive Notice: Notice imparted by the public records of the county when documents are recorded.

Conveyance: An instrument in writing, such as a deed or trust deed, used to transfer (convey) title to property from one person to another.

Corporation: An entity authorized by law and established by a group of people, the stockholders, which is endowed with certain rights, privileges, and duties similar to those of an individual.

Covenant: (1) A formal agreement or contract between two parties in which one party gives the other certain promises and assurances, such as the covenant of warranty in a warranty deed. (2) Agreements or promises contained in deeds and other instruments for performance or nonperformance of certain acts, or use or nonuse of property in a certain manner.

Covenants, Conditions and Restrictions: Commonly called "CC & Rs" the term usually refers to a written recorded declaration which sets forth certain covenants, conditions, restrictions, rules, or regulations established by a subdivider or other landowner to create uniformity of buildings and use within tracts of land or groups of lots. The restrictions also can be established by deed. CC & Rs are sometimes referred to as private zoning.

Deed: Written document by which an estate or interest in real property is transferred from one person to another. The person who transfers the interest is called the "grantor." The one who acquires the interest is called the "grantee." Examples of deeds are grant deeds, administrators' deeds, executors' deeds, quitclaim deeds, etc. The deed to use depends on the language of the deed, the legal capacity of the grantor, and other circumstances.

Deed of Trust or Trust Deed: A written document by which the title to land is conveyed as security for the repayment of a loan or other obligation. It is a form of mortgage. The landowner or debtor is called the "trustor." The party to whom the legal title is conveyed is the "trustee." The lender is the "beneficiary."

Deed Restrictions: Limitations in the deed to a property that dictate certain uses that may or not be made of the property.

Defective Title: (1) Title to a negotiable instrument obtained by fraud. (2) Title to real property that lacks some of the elements necessary to transfer good title.

Demand Note: A note having no date for repayment, but due on demand of the lender.

Description: The exact location of a piece of real property stated in terms of lot, block, tract, part lot, metes and bounds, recorded instruments, or U.S. government survey (sectionalized). This is also referred to as the "legal description" of a property.

Earnest Money Deposit: Down payment made by a purchaser of real estate as evidence of good faith; a deposit or partial payment.

Easement: A right or interest in the use of the land of another that entitles the holder to some use, privilege, or benefit, such as to place pole lines, pipelines, or roads. A right of way giving persons other than the owner access to or over a property.

Eminent Domain: The right of a government to take privately owned property for public purposes under condemnation proceedings upon payment of its reasonable value. (See also: Condemnation.)

Encroachment: The presence of an improvement such as a building, a wall, a fence, or other fixture that overlaps onto the property of an adjoining owner.

Encumbrance: A right or claim upon real property held by someone other than the property owner. Encumbrances are divided into two classes: liens (mortgages, deeds of trust, mechanics' liens, local taxes, assessments, judgments, attachments, etc.) and encumbrances other than liens, which are limitations on the ownership of the land (resticttions, reservations, easements, etc.).

Endorsement: Addition to or modification of a title insurance policy that expands or changes coverage of the policy, fulfilling specific requirements of the insured.

Equity: The market value of real property, less the amount of existing liens.

Equity Financing: The act of raising money for company activities by selling common or preferred stock to individual or institutional investors. In return for the money paid, shareholders receive ownership interests in the corporation. Also known as "share capital."

Escrow: An independent third party who acts as the agent for buyer and seller or for borrower and lender, carrying out instructions of both and disbursing documents and funds.

Estate: (1) The interest or nature of the interest a person has in property, such as a life estate, the estate of a deceased person. (2) A large house with substantial grounds surrounding it, giving the connotation of belonging to a wealthy person.

Estoppel Certificate: A tenant estoppel certificate is used to identify the tenant and landlord, the location of the property, the date the tenant signed the lease, and other information pertinent to the sale of a property. An estoppel certificate confirms the status of all leases in the property and whether any tenants have claims against the landlord that might offset future rent payments.

Execution: An order directing a sheriff, constable, marshal or court-appointed commissioner to enforce a money judgment against the property of a debtor. This officer, if necessary, may sell the property to satisfy the judgment.

Executor, Executrix: A person appointed in a will and affirmed by the probate court to cause a distribution of the decedent's estate in accordance with the will. (The one who makes the will is called a "testator.")

Fee Simple: An estate under which the owner is entitled to unrestricted powers to dispose of the property, and which can be left by will or inherited. Commonly used as a synonym for ownership.

File and Use: In most states, title insurers file rate schedules, title insurance policies, and endorsement forms with the State Insurance Department or other state agency and then may use such items or rates starting within a specified period of time after filing. Rates so filed usually are mandatory.

Fixed Rate Mortgage: A mortgage having a rate of interest that remains the same for the life of the mortgage.

Foreclosure: The sale of property used as security for a debt after default in payment. The legal process by which a borrower in default under a mortgage is deprived of his or her interest in the mortgaged property. This usually involves a forced sale of the property at public auction with the proceeds of the sale being applied to the mortgage debt.

Forfeiture of Title: A common penalty for the violation of conditions or restrictions imposed by the seller upon the buyer in a deed or other proper document. For example, a deed may be granted upon the condition that if liquor is sold on the land, the title to the land will be forfeited (that is, lost) by the buyer (or some later owner) and will revert to the seller.

Full Disclosure: In real estate, revealing all the known facts that may affect the decision of a buyer or tenant. A broker must disclose known defects in the property for sale or lease.

"Good Faith" or "Mortgage Savings" Clause: A clause in CC & Rs providing that "a violation thereof shall not defeat or render invalid the lien of any mortgage or deed of trust made in good faith and for value."

Good Faith Purchaser or Mortgagee: A person who buys or lends in good faith, that is, without notice of any existing problem, where value is paid or lent.

GP (General Partnership): A business with two or more partners in which all are liable for any of its obligations. There is no limited liability in a general partnership.

Grant Deed: One of the many types of deeds used to transfer real property. Contains warranties against prior conveyances or encumbrances. When title insurance is purchased, warranties in a deed are of little practical significance.

Gross Multiplier: A factor used to multiply the gross income of a property to determine an acceptable price.

Hazard Insurance: Real estate insurance protecting against fire, some natural causes, vandalism, etc., depending upon the policy. An owner often adds liability insurance and extended coverage for personal property.

Homestead: A statutory protection from execution or the establishment of title by occupation of real property in accordance with the laws of various states or the federal government.

Impounds: A trust type of account established by lenders for the accumulation of borrower's funds to meet periodic payments of taxes, mortgage insurance premiums, and/or future insurance policy premiums. Lenders require it under certain circumstances to protect their security interest in a property.

Internal Rate of Return: The average yearly return on an investment during the holding period. The Internal Rate of Return can be calculateed before or after taxation. I personally never calculate the taxation, because I tell my investors that my job is to make them money; their CPA or tax lawyer should help them with taxation.

Indemnity: Insurance against possible loss or damage. A title insurance policy is a contract of indemnity.

Judgment Lien: A lien against the property of a judgment debtor. It is an involuntary lien.

Land Contract: An installment contract for the sale of land whereby the seller holds legal title and the buyer has equitable title until the sales price is paid in full.

Lease: An agreement by which an owner of real property (leaser) gives the right of possession to another (lessee), for a specified period of time (term) and for a specified consideration (rent).

Legal Description: A description of land recognized by law, based on government surveys, spelling out the exact boundaries of the entire piece of land. It should so thoroughly identify a parcel of land that it cannot be confused with any other.

Lender: Any person or entity advancing funds to be repaid. Also a general term encompassing all mortgagees and beneficiaries under deeds of trust.

Lien: An encumbrance against property for money, either voluntary or involuntary. All liens are encumbrances, but not all encumbrances are liens. A legal claim against a property that must be paid off when the property is sold. A mortgage or first trust deed is considered a lien.

LLC (Limited Liability Company): A business entity under which the owners are not personally liable for debts or other business liabilities.

LP (Limited Partnership): A business with a general partner who runs the business and assumes its debts and obligations and at least one limited partner. Limited partners are not liable for the obligations of the business, although they have rights to the partnership's cash flow.

Mechanic's Lien: A lien created by statute for the purpose of securing priority of payment for the price or value of work performed and materials furnished in construction or repair of improvements to land, and which attaches to the land as well as the improvements.

Mezzanine or "Bridge" Financing: A loan given to buyers or the owners of a property to complete a purchase or to rehab, remodel, or convert a property to a different use in order to maximize its value. The term of the loan is typically three to thirty-six months. Quite often mezzanine lenders, in addition to charging a higher interest rate and upfront fees, also take a percentage of the profits. They also may want to oversee and approve how the money is spent.

MLS: Multiple Listing Service. A service available to real estate agents for listing and viewing property for sale or lease as well as researching comparable property values within a neighborhood.

Mortgage: (1) To hypothecate as security, real property for the payment of a debt. The borrower (mortgagor) retains possession and use of the property. (2) The instrument by which real estate is hypothecated as security for the repayment of a loan.

Net Operating Income (NOI): The rental income of a property after operating expenses, including maintenance, janitorial, supplies, insurance, accounting, management, etc.

Note (Promissory Note): A unilateral agreement containing an express and absolute promise of the signer to pay to a named person, or order, or bearer, a definite sum of money at a specified date or on demand. Usually provides for interest and, concerning real property, is secured by a mortgage or trust deed.

Original Cost: The purchase price of property, paid by the present owner. The present owner may or may not be the first owner.

Owner's Policy: A policy of title insurance usually insuring an owner of real estate against loss occasioned by defects in, liens against, or unmarketable nature of the owner's title.

Parcel: Any area of land contained within a single description.

Partnership: An association of two or more persons who have contracted to join in business and share the profits.

Personal Property (movable): Any property that is not designated by law as real property (i.e., money, goods, evidences of debt, rights of action, furniture, automobiles).

PITI: A payment that combines Principal, Interest, Taxes, and Insurance.

PLAT: A plan, map, or chart of a tract or town site dividing a parcel of land into lots.

Power of Attorney: A document by which one person (called the "principal") authorizes another person (called the "attorney-in-fact") to act for him/her in a specific manner in designated transactions.

Preliminary Report (Pre, Prelim): A written report issued by a title company preliminary to issuing title insurance showing the recorded condition of title of the property in question. (See also: Commitment.)

Priority: The order of preference, rank or position of the various liens and encumbrances affecting the title to a particular parcel of land. Usually the date and time of recording determine the relative priority between documents.

Public Domain: Land owned by the government and belonging to the community at large.

Quitclaim Deed: A deed operating as a release; intended to pass any title, interest, or claim the grantor may have in the property, but not containing any warranty of a valid interest or title in the grantor.

Quiet Title: To free the title to a piece of land from the claims of other persons by means of a court action called a "quiet title" action. The court decree obtained is a "quiet title" decree.

Real Property (immovable): Land, from the center of the earth and extending above the surface indefinitely, including all inherent natural attributes and any man-made improvements of a permanent nature, such as minerals, trees, or buildings.

Reconveyance: An instrument used to transfer title from a trustee to the owner of real estate, when title is held as collateral security for a debt. Most commonly used upon payment in full of a trust deed. Also called a deed of reconveyance or release.

Recording: Filing documents affecting real property as a matter of public record, giving notice to future purchasers, creditors, or other interested parties. Recording is controlled by statute and usually requires the witnessing and notarizing of an instrument to be recorded.

Recourse: Recourse refers to a loan backed by a personal guarantee, meaning that a lender can require borrowers to pay back the loan with personal assets.

Reinsurance: A contract that one insurer makes with another to protect the first insurer, wholly or partially, against loss or liability by reason of a risk under a separate and distinct contract as insurer of a third party. Reinsurance differs from coinsurance in that only one insurer has a direct contractual relationship with the insured.

Restrictions: Often called restrictive covenants. Provisions in a deed or other instrument whereby an owner of land prohibits or restricts certain use, occupation, or improvement of the land.

Right of Way: (1) The right to pass over property owned by another, usually based upon an easement. (2) A path or thoroughfare over which passage is made. (3) A strip of land over which facilities such as highways, railroads, or power lines are built.

Sale and Leaseback A situation in which the grantor in a deed to a parcel of property sells it and retains possession by simultaneously leasing it from the grantee.

Search: A careful exploration and examination of the public records in an effort to find all recorded instruments relating to a particular chain of title.

Separate Property: Real property owned by one spouse exclusive of any interest of the other spouse.

Street Improvement Bonds: Interest-bearing bonds issued, usually by a city or county, to secure the payment of assessments levied against land to pay for street improvements.

Subdivision: An area of land laid out and divided into lots, blocks, and building sites, and in which public facilities are laid out, such as streets, alleys, parks, and easements for public utilities.

Subordination Agreement: An agreement by which one encumbrance (for example, a mortgage) is made subject to another encumbrance (perhaps a lease). To "subordinate" is to "make subject to" or to make of lower priority.

Survey: The measurement by a surveyor of real property defining the boundaries of a parcel of land.

Syndicator: One who syndicates, or pools, group investments to buy real estate.

Syndication: The pooling or grouping of investments in order to buy real estate.

Tax Deed: A deed executed by the tax collector to the state, county, or city when no redemption is made from a tax sale.

Tax Sale: Property sold by a taxing authority or the court in order to recover delinquent taxes.

Tenants in Common: An undivided interest in property, not necessarily equal, held by two or more persons. There is no right of survivorship upon death of one or more of the tenants in common.

Title: (1) A combination of all the elements that constitute a legal right to own, possess, use, control, enjoy, and dispose of real estate or a right or interest therein. (2) The rights of ownership recognized and protected by the law.

Title Insurance: Insured statement of the condition of title or ownership of real property. For a one-time-only premium, the named insured and their heirs are protected against title defects, liens, and encumbrances existing as of the date of the policy. In the event of a claim, the title company provides legal defense from the policyholder and pays any covered losses incurred as a result of such claim.

Title Report: See Preliminary Report.

Title Search: A review of all recorded documents affecting a specific parcel of land to determine the present condition of title. An experienced title officer or attorney reviews and analyzes all material relating to the search, then determines the sufficiency and status of title for insurance of a title insurance policy.

Unlawful Detainer: An instrument filed with the court when a landlord wishes to evict a tenant for non-payment of rent or for endangering the safety of the other tenants or property.

Variable Interest Rate: An interest rate that fluctuates with the current cost of money; subject to adjustment if the prevailing rate moves up or down.

Vendor's Lien: An implied lien given by law to a vendor for the remaining unpaid and unsecured part of a purchase price.

Venue: Neighborhood; often used to refer to the county or place in which an acknowledgment is made before a notary; also refers to the county in which a lawsuit may be filed or tried.

Vesting: The names, status, and manner in which title of ownership is held with a fixed or determinable interest in a particular parcel of real property; also that portion of a title report or policy setting forth the above.

Waive: To voluntarily and intentionally relinquish a known right, claim, or privilege.

Warranty Deed: A deed used in many states to convey fee title to real property.

ABOUT THE AUTHOR

Karim Jaude, your partner in real estate, has founded and operated nineteen successful companies.

He made his first $1 million by the age of twenty-six, by buying and fixing up distressed properties and businesses.

For the last forty-five years, Karim has developed, invested, financed, brokered, managed, and consulted in real estate properties in eight countries.

These properties have ranged from single family homes to condo projects and apartment buildings, from shopping centers to commercial and industrial buildings, from hotels to land, and from mixed-use to special-use properties.

He has built from scratch, remodeled, fixed up, and converted properties for different uses, in order to maximize the return on his investments. In 1984 he was the very first to convert an industrial building in downtown Los Angeles into artist lofts. His offices have handled more that $20 billion in real estate transactions.

Karim mentors, writes, teaches, and speaks about real estate frequently. He has been published in more than 115 business and real estate publications nationwide, as well as in 42 newsletters.

Karim enjoys tennis, skiing, reading, and traveling, and is passionate about helping others.

Most importantly, for almost forty years, Karim has committed—and never failed—to help at least one person every single day.

www.ingramcontent.com/pod-product-compliance
Lightning Source LLC
Chambersburg PA
CBHW031241090426
42742CB00007B/273